Systemic Team Coaching

John Leary-Joyce

Hilary Lines

Systemic Team Coaching® is a registered trademark with the Academy of Executive Coaching to ensure that anyone using it adheres broadly to the framework and principles outlined in this book.

An Imprint of: Academy of Executive Coaching Ltd.

64 Warwick Road

St Albans

Herts

AL1 4DL

HYPERLINK "http: //www.aoec.com"

www.aoec.com

info@aoec.com

First published in Great Britain in 2018

©John Leary-Joyce, Hilary Lines 2018

ISBN: 978-D-993D772-2-7

Cover design Simon Moss

www.theanswermachine.co.uk

Typesetting and figures

chriscraddock@sky.com

Contents

About the Authors...iv

In The Beginning...vi

Introduction by Peter Hawkins...viii

Chapter 1 – What is Systemic Team Coaching®?................................1

Chapter 2 – Why Become a Systemic Team Coach?...........................11

Chapter 3 – The Five Disciplines Framework....................................19

Chapter 4 – The Systemic Team Coaching® Process........................35

Chapter 5 – Developing Yourself as a Systemic Team Coach 59

Chapter 6 – Leadership and Systemic Relationships....................................77

Chapter 7 – Your Route to Becoming a Systemic Team Coach........................91

References

Index...105

Appendix i Tools & Techniques Resource....................................111

Appendix ii Team Connect 360 survey tool.................................116

Appendix iii Semi Structured Inquiry Questions............................117

About the Authors

John Leary-Joyce

As entrepreneurial founder and Executive Chair of AoEC John understands the importance of teamwork and the value of team coaching. Over the last 20 years he has become widely recognised as a senior transformational coach, combining this with an initial 20-year career as a Gestalt psychotherapist, group facilitator and trainer. He is also the author of the highly acclaimed book *The Fertile Void, Gestalt Coaching at Work*, a practical and effective methodology for individual and team coaching.

With substantial team building and OD experience, he has become regarded as one of the top team coaches working in large organisations, especially in legal and accountancy firms.

He is senior faculty on the innovative Master Practitioner Diploma in Systemic Team Coaching® programme which he co-designed with Peter Hawkins and Hilary Lines and delivers worldwide.

He has an MA in Executive Coaching, is an accredited coach with APECS, and ICF PCC, a qualified supervisor and frequent international conference presenter. His other passion is dancing the Tango, which he relates closely to leadership, coaching and teamwork.

Dr Hilary Lines

Is an executive and team coach, leadership consultant and educator, with over 30 years' experience of working with senior executives in a range of sectors across the globe. A driving force for her work lies in her belief that leaders in complex organisations create value through working constructively with difference at the 'touchpoint' of their connection with others. She helps her clients look in depth at how they can bring the best of themselves to their leadership relationships, how they sometimes jeopardise their own impact, and how they can enhance and expand their individual and collective leadership presence and impact through developing greater relational agility, resilience and authenticity.

Her 2013 book *Touchpoint Leadership* (co-authored with Jacqui Scholes-Rhodes) describes how she applies her model of leadership to her coaching, team coaching and consulting practice.

Hilary co-leads the Academy of Executive Coaching Master Practitioner Programme in Systemic Team Coaching® and is a respected supervisor of practising team coaches. She is also a faculty member of the Teleos Leadership Institute's Coach Development Programme, based in Philadelphia. She is an ICF accredited PCC coach and a registered Analytic-Network coach.

Prior to setting up her own business, Hilary led partner and leadership development for PwC Consulting worldwide.

Professor Peter Hawkins – Primary Contributor

Honorary President AoEC, Professor of Leadership Henley Business School, Founder and Emeritus Chair, Bath Consultancy Group, Chair Renewal Associates, The Centre for Supervision and Team Development (Bath) and Metaco (South Africa).

He is a leading consultant, writer and researcher in leadership and leadership development and an international thought leader in executive coaching, team coaching and coaching supervision.

Over the last 30 years he has worked with many leading companies in many parts of the world, coaching Boards and Leadership Teams. He co-designed the AoEC Systemic Team Coaching® Diploma and is now visiting faculty.

Author of several best-selling books, primarily *Leadership Team Coaching and Leadership Team Coaching in Practice* which are the foundations for this book.

In The Beginning

Systemic Team Coaching® is the brainchild of Peter Hawkins.

In one of those amazing synchronistic events I (John) was chatting with Peter at a coaching conference in 2008 about the limits of individual coaching and a desire to get back to working with teams. Peter informed me that he was in the process of researching and writing a new book: *Leadership Team Coaching.* The aim was to bring together 70 years of best practice in Organisation and Team development with the best of the relational and change processes, including coaching from the last 30 years. (Hawkins and Shohet 1989, 2000; Hawkins and Smith 2006). He wanted his work to fill a critical need for trained professionals who can enable sustained change by coaching teams across nested systemic levels. To this end he was looking for a way to test out and help develop his ideas in practice.

As CEO of the Academy of Executive Coaching, this was a brilliant opportunity to partner with Peter in creating a new field of Team Coaching. With Marion Gillie, senior faculty at AoEC, we set about establishing a pioneer Systemic Team Coaching® training group.

Hilary Lines and Gil Schwenk joined us in developing a one year training programme based around Peter's fledgling idea of the Five Disciplines model for high performing teams. Designing a programme with new theoretical ideas using well tried coaching principles and building an innovative and experiential methodology was an exciting and demanding challenge.

We presented our ideas at conferences, introductory events and one day workshops and were astonished at the huge positive response. Clearly the one-to-one coaching market was thirsty for team coaching.

In September 2010 we launched our pioneer residential Systemic Team Coaching® programme with 16 adventurous souls: Sharon Toye; Oliver Strachan; Philip Pirie; Sue Coyne; Judith Nicol; Kevin Greenleaves; Alison Hogan; Vicki Masters; Marianne Skelcher; Nicola Haskins; Donna Dibbert; Elke Anderson; Jill Fairbairns; Margot Corbin; Darryl Stevens; Richard Clarke - with seven client teams willing to be guinea pigs for Systemic Team Coaching® practice: One World Action; Addleshaws; Bentley; Brent CC; Manchester Airport Authority; Skanska; Water Aid.

True to the principles of Systemic Team Coaching®, we all experimented a lot and learned a vast amount. At the time of writing and through multiple iterations we are on to Systemic Team Coaching® Diploma programme 6 and have created a short impactful 3 day Certificate programme (see Chapter 7 for details).

® AoEC have obtained a Registered Trademark on the title Systemic Team Coaching® to ensure that anyone using it adheres broadly to the framework and principles outlined in this book.

1. Hawkins, P. *(2011, 2nd edition 2014, 3rd edition 2017) Leadership Team Coaching: Developing Collective Transformational Leadership.* London, Kogan Page.

Introduction to Systemic Team Coaching®

Professor Peter Hawkins.

There is an abundance of good coaches, team facilitators, organisational consultants, counsellors and psychotherapists in the world, but what is desperately needed are professionals who can draw on all these skills to enable profound and sustainable systemic change. This means change within and between the nested systemic levels of the Individual, Team, Business Function, Organisational Stakeholders and Wider Eco-system.

The future is bigger and more challenging than any of us can grasp or address, alone or in groups. The challenges will take all of us, yes, all seven billion of us working together to address – and this will require new human levels of empathy, systemic thinking, collaboration and teamwork. Many are recognising that global companies, if they can get free of the magnetic pull to focus on short-term quarterly profits and the overwhelming deluge of daily issues and problems, have an enormous power to lead breakthrough change in the world and thus to help us address the myriad of challenges that we face.

This is where leadership teams have an enormous responsibility, for they can act as an accelerator, brake or even derailer of change and adaptation in their organisation and the wider business eco-system.

$$1 + 1 + 1 + 1 + 1 = 2$$

In my forty years of working with leadership teams, I have often found that the average intelligence of the individual team members was over 120, but the collective intelligence of the team as a whole was about 60. There is a great need to help teams develop generative ways of working so they function at more than the sum of their parts.

$$1 + 1 + 1 + 1 + 1 = 12$$

This requires every team member to take responsibility for their individual part as well as for the functioning of the whole team, representing their collective purpose and objectives to the myriad of external stakeholders. It is also essential that it is a learning team, where members are jointly and individually developing and adapting to the ever-increasing speed of change. For we have entered a VUCA (Volatile, Uncertain, Complex and Ambiguous) world; a time of hyper-velocity change, in technology, globalization, climate change, economic turbulence, and organisational evolution. A world where the major challenges can no longer be solved by 'heroic leaders' or even nation states. As I said above, the need for collective leadership and collaborative ways of working across organisational, sectorial and national boundaries has never been greater.

Coaching has achieved much in the last 30 years. One of its greatest has been to move the emphasis of leadership development from an over-emphasis on I.Q. to the need to develop E.Q. (Emotional Intelligence). The need in the 21st Century is to go further and help leaders develop 'We Q' or collaborative intelligence, which is essential if teams are going to step up to the challenge and be more than the sum of their parts. You cannot learn 'We Q' individually, only collectively, as it resides in the relationships between team members and between the team and its stakeholders.

Systemic Team Coaching® is an approach I have developed over the last 30 years with the help of many colleagues, in particular Hilary Lines and John Leary-Joyce. We have brought together the best practice which has evolved over the last 70 years from the fields of Organisation and Team Development and linked that with the best of the relational and change processes from the last thirty years in coaching[1].

For too long we believed that if team members got on well together and acted as 'a team' it would be effective, but numerous researchers have shown that in fact a group of individuals working alongside each other are more effective than a pseudo team – one that goes through the motions of being a team, but lacks true shared purpose. They have also shown that relating well together is not enough – the three biggest factors in teams creating value are:

- That the team has a clear collective purpose and agreed objectives (Clarifying Discipline)
- That these are aligned to the needs of all their stakeholders (Commissioning Discipline)
- They all recognise that this can only be achieved by effective team collaboration (Co-creating Discipline).

These three disciplines of high performing teams are the pre-requisites, but real value is only created when these foundations are converted into transforming the relationships with all the team's stakeholders (Connecting Discipline). Furthermore, it only becomes sustainable if the team is constantly learning and adapting (Core Learning Discipline).

In our Systemic Team Coaching® approach we have drawn upon many coaching and consulting methods and processes. These include ways of contracting, inquiry questioning, 360° feedback and facilitating interventions which we have applied to our work with teams. In this book, Hilary and John not only provide an overview of these key foundational models, disciplines and processes but they also illustrate these with a range of very useful short vignettes and examples that bring the practice to life on to the page.

When individually coaching CEOs and other senior leaders, we find that one of the most frequent issues they bring to coaching is how they may develop and coach their team so that they take more responsibility for collective and effective leadership. This involves us in supervising the way in which they lead their teams. To do this effectively as individual coaches, we need to understand the principles of both supervision and Systemic Team Coaching.® Therefore, we increasingly believe both subjects need to be addressed as part of every coach training programme, as it is in the Systemic Team Coaching® programmes that we deliver at the Academy of Executive Coaching.

Hilary and John draw on their in-depth skills and knowledge as team coaches as well as their experience of teaching and supervising people across the world through their Systemic Team Coaching® training programmes. The book therefore provides a clear and concise introduction to Systemic Team Coaching® from two of the most experienced international trainers and team coaching supervisors in the field. It is particularly written for those who are already experienced individual coaches and who now want to extend their practice into working with teams and wider systems.

Even if you only coach one-to-one, you will sooner or later find yourself indirectly working with teams, organisations and wider systems. This is because individual coaches do not just bring themselves to their coaching, but also the dynamics of the teams they lead and work within, the organisational culture they are part of, and the wider eco-systems they inhabit.

Our hope is that this book will encourage more and more coaches to step bravely into the exciting and rewarding world of Systemic Team Coaching® and fill the global need for trained professionals who can enable profound change across the connected nested systemic levels.

1. Hawkins and Shohet 1989, 2000; Hawkins and Smith 2006 and 2013, Hawkins 2011, 2014, 2014b, 2017, Hawkins, Leary-Joyce and Lines 2016.

1

WHAT IS SYSTEMIC TEAM COACHING®?

Questions covered in this chapter

- What is a team and how is it different from a group?
- What is Systemic Team Coaching® and how is it different?
- How does a systemic team coach view the team?

The difference between a team and a group

While there is much semantic discussion about the differences between a team and a group, there is one important distinction between a team and a working group that helps us clarify the focus and scope of the practice of Systemic Team Coaching.®

Primarily, a team has a collective purpose and objective which its members are jointly responsible for fulfilling. This means that they are dependent on each other for the achievement of the objective and that ignoring this interdependence will make them less effective.

While a working group does usually have a collective purpose – a reason why they have joined together - each group member is individually responsible for delivering his or her own objectives. The group normally serves the purpose of providing coordination, information sharing, consultation, learning or support to its members, often led by a co-ordinator, facilitator, manager or leader.

The definition by Katzenbach and Smith[1] is helpful here:

" A team is

- a small number of people

- with complimentary skills

- who are committed to a common purpose and set of performance goals

- and an approach for which they hold themselves mutually accountable."

(Katzenbach & Smith, 2009)

The systemic team coach therefore needs to be concerned not only with helping the team optimise the way it is communicating and learning together (the work of a group) but with enabling the team to define and execute its collective task in a way that creates greater value than possible from the sum of the individual members.

Peter Hawkins[2] develops this further:

"...a high performing team: effectively meets and communicates in a way that raises morale and alignment, engages with all the team's key stakeholder groups in a way that grows performance and provides constant learning and development for all its members and the collective team."

(Hawkins, 2011)

1. Katzenbach, John R and Smith, Douglas K, *The Discipline of Teams*, Harvard Business Review Classics, 2009

2.Hawkins P, *Leadership Team Coaching*, Kogan Page, Chapter 2, 2017

What is Systemic Team Coaching® and how is it different?

We have defined Systemic Team Coaching® as:

A process of coaching the whole team both together and apart, over a designated period of time to enable it to

- Align on common purpose
- Collaborate and learn across diversity
- Develop collective leadership
- Achieve performance objectives
- Effectively engage with their key stakeholder groups
- Jointly transform the wider business.

(Leary-Joyce, Lines & Hawkins 2014)[3]

It is evident from this definition that the term Systemic Team Coaching® draws on a range of approaches and skills relevant to adult and organisational learning. Rather than talking about its difference from other approaches, we find it more helpful to consider how Systemic Team Coaching® draws on those approaches to create a new multidisciplinary approach which consists of:

Individual Coaching. The concept in coaching of the client being 'resourceful and whole', and therefore able, with client-centered support, to develop new thinking and capability to grow and develop is also core to Systemic Team Coaching®. The difference is that the Systemic Team Coaching® approach is applied to the team as a collective entity. That said, the Systemic Team Coaching® approach is normally incomplete without the systemic team coach coaching at least the team leader and often the team members too (see later chapter). So being an experienced coach is a pre-requisite to being a systemic team coach.

Group Coaching. This is defined as coaching a group of managers or leaders who have a shared interest in a project or issue but no collective responsibility for an output. Here they can address the common issues that they share to seek individual solutions and actions. The group coach has to be able to facilitate the discussion, supporting and challenging members to engage in dialogue rather than just direct and tell, working in a way that enables the group to learn and develop – skills that are essential to the systemic team coach. A similar approach called Action Learning Sets was created by Reg Revens[4] in the 1980s.

3. Adapted from Peter Hawkins, *Leadership Team Coaching*, p 78, 2017
4. Revans R, *ABC of Action Learning*, Gower Publishing, 2016

Team building. This normally refers to a set of activities designed to help a team in the early stages of team development or at a key transition point, to build awareness of its members, their styles, roles and preferences so that they can work more effectively together. The ability to help team members share and appreciate their differences and to work effectively with those differences is a core skill of a systemic team coach. Unlike team building events or away-days, however, this skill is interwoven within the Systemic Team Coaching® process.

Team Facilitation. This is a process by which a facilitator, leader or moderator manages the process of team work, so that the members of a meeting can concentrate on the task. This again is a core skill through which a systemic team coach enables a team to work and learn together. However, the coach needs to ensure that, in her endeavor to help the team process, she does not step into the middle of important operational discussion between team members. The focus must be on enabling the team to produce an output, not on the delivery of the output per se.

Inter-Team Coaching. This facilitates the clarification of how a range of teams within an organisational system connect and maximize their communication and co-operation. This may involve bringing representatives together from each team, for example financial directors from each division, into a group coaching context to learn and develop with and from each other. It can also involve the systemic team coach in bringing teams together to look at their relationships, how far this serves common stakeholder needs and how they need to partner more effectively to meet those needs. This helps the systemic team coach to maintain an overall perspective on the mutual stakeholder relationships.[5]

Organisational Development is described by the Chartered Institute of Personnel and Development (CIPD) as a planned and systematic approach to enabling sustained organisation performance through the involvement of its people. It is otherwise described as an organisation-wide approach to achieve sustained change in the alignment of strategy, structure, process, people and culture. Systemic Team Coaching® does not start organisation-wide, it starts with the team. It involves working with a team in a way that helps the team

---

5. The importance, in complex contexts, of working at the interface between teams and improving the way they serve multiple stakeholder interests is compellingly addressed in McChrystal, General Stanley, *Team of Teams: new rules of engagement for a complex world*, Penguin Random House, 2015

optimise not just its internal performance but the way it engages its diverse stakeholders. This does require us to pay attention to wider organisational strategy, to existing and aspired culture, and to processes which will support leadership and engagement. It requires us to stand back and see the connected whole, and to enable the team to do that too. The next section will tell you more about what we mean.

How does a Systemic Team Coach view the team? The Six Lenses

We use the term 'Systemic' to refer to the multi-layered perspective the team coach needs to adopt in order to see a fuller and more complex picture of the team in its context. Of course, the more complex it is, the more confusing and therefore the more difficult it is to choose a way forward or make interventions.

This complexity means that we have to leave a linear, clean, simple approach behind and begin to see patterns, shapes and influences and recognise that everything is interconnected.

In the diagram below (Fig. 1.1) we've identified six levels to illustrate the structure, but in reality they interweave and merge together and are present and constantly moving at the same time. Our challenge is to be aware of all the potential options to make choices and decisions on interventions. That's why we call these levels the 'lenses' of a systemic team coach.

Fig. 1.1: The 6 Lenses of Systemic Team Coaching®

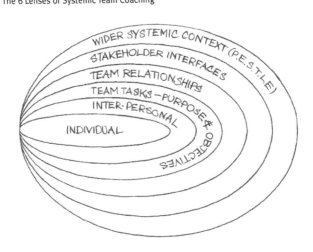

The importance of holding these Six Lenses is illustrated by the following story.

I get a call from the Company Chair with whom I've worked before, asking if I can provide executive coaching for a new executive, Jane, who has recently joined the senior management team and is not fitting in well. On the face of it, and from the point of view of the **first lens** this looks like a standard individual coaching assignment that I'd be happy to undertake.

As usual my process is to have the chemistry session to meet Jane, identify the issues and understand what the work with her would be like if she is going to creatively adapt to the new organisation and team that she is faced with.

However, on understanding more about the situation and context of the assignment I'm thinking that her issues are a symptom of a much wider systemic malaise.

The individual coaching process also involves the **second lens** of the six: interpersonal relationships, and a three way session with Jane and her team leader. This gives me more data on the context Jane is working in and clarifies that there are some interpersonal difficulties between them. Having done mediation and couples coaching I suggest that it would be most helpful if we do a few joint sessions and utilise the personality profiling data that they have available to explore their different working styles.

As we engage in these joint sessions it becomes clear that the conflict between them is mirrored in the relationships between other team members. At this point there is a decision to be made: either I continue with this assignment as an individual coaching issue, with the coachee as the 'problem', or I seek to widen the scope of the work into a team development intervention.

On discussion with the team leader it is agreed to organise a two day team-building session where the themes that occurred between the pair were addressed as a whole team issue: **lens three**. This is duly organised and a productive day ensues. However, the main issue to arise is not a personality clash or poor working relationships but that there is a lack of clarity about the purpose and direction of the team. This has given rise to team members going off and working on different aspects of the business and feeling frustrated that others are not 'on board'. What became clear is that Jane, the new team member, has been impatient with this approach and had been complaining to the Chair about lack of business leadership.

The most fruitful intervention now is to work on creating a shared purpose and 'joint endeavour' with the team. It is well known from research (Katzenbach & Smith) that if a team is co-ordinated and collaborates to achieve a compelling vision, purpose and objectives then they will overcome many personality difficulties and differences. At this point it becomes clear that this is moving into a Systemic Team Coaching® intervention – although in this case the sponsor is not willing to commit to a longer term relationship. What they ask is for me to facilitate an off-site session to help the team address strategy and objectives together and thrash out a common purpose and joint objectives: **lens four**.

This meeting highlights the general frustration in the whole team that they are not clear what priorities the board actually want them to focus on. A lot of room has been left for interpretation by individual team members, who have been pursuing a direction that suited them personally and professionally. Conflict and competition for resources has inevitably arisen creating a silo mentality and a focus on personal prestige. There is a collective realisation that they can't effectively progress as a united team until they have 'interrogated' the board and other key stakeholders on what outcomes they expect from the senior management team. We proceed to look at the various stakeholders and identify what they may need from the senior management team. Each team member takes away the task to gather this data and reconvene in a month to share the results.

It is also confirmed that I'll lead a group coaching session between a sub-set of the team and the Chair plus two other board members to discuss what they want and what is realistic to achieve: **lens five**.

This meeting is duly convened and a difficult but rich exchange ensues. What emerges is that a number of major regulatory changes are afoot in the wider profession and the board is also concerned about global financial trends. This has given rise to splits at board level and a lack of clarity about what direction they want the senior management team to move in. Our new team member, Jane, had a previous role in regularity authority so has been badgering the Chair to attend to the changes she knew were imminent.

The output from this group coaching session is that a special task force is to be set up to research into the implications of the potential changes. This group will feed back the results to the board. The board will then make key strategic decisions and give a clear direction to the senior management team on what they are required to do: **lens six**.

Having come this far together, the sponsor and team leader see the value of engaging in a Systemic Team Coaching® process over the next year to consolidate the learning and embed new processes and outputs.

Now reflect back on this story

What if the coach had stuck with coaching in the lens they were familiar with? Yes, undoubtedly some progress would have been made in a limited way but by ranging up through the systemic lenses and then back down again, the team achieves success in the direction that is required with the most efficient level of integrated energy.

As systemic team coaches we have to stay aware of all six lenses and guide our client to also attend to each of them, so there is the focus on the level that will give the greatest benefit to the team and the organisation it is serving.

Of course, most systemic team work does not evolve from a single one-to-one coaching request, as in this story. It is far more common for a team leader or other organisational sponsor to identify a development need in a team, and then the systemic team coach's task is to understand where support is needed, down into the interpersonal circles and out into the wider contextual circles. We will talk later about how Systemic Team Coaching® assignments arise and what are the first steps that you take as a systemic team coach.

Reflect now on where you are most comfortable working in the six lenses and where the biggest challenge will lie for you in working across them.

Think about how you and your clients might benefit from your developing skills and expertise in Systemic Team Coaching® We will share our own stories and our thinking on this question in Chapter 2.

Summary

- It is important to be clear about the difference between a group and a team – this will influence the approach you use as a coach

- Systemic Team Coaching® draws on a range of approaches to form a programme of work in which the systemic team coach partners with the team over a period of time, working with them when they are together and when they are apart.

- The systemic team coach views the team through the six lenses and adapts and flexes his coaching approach in order to provide greatest value to the team and system in which it lives. These lenses are:

  1. Individual
  2. Interpersonal
  3. Team Relationships
  4. Team Tasks
  5. Stakeholder Interface
  6. Wider Organisational Context.

2

WHY BE INTERESTED IN SYSTEMIC TEAM COACHING®?

Questions covered in this chapter

- What does becoming a systemic team coach mean for the coach?
- Why would a team leader be interested?
- Why would a team be interested?

From our experience in working with teams and in training and supervising others who work with teams, we believe there are three high level shifts that the coach needs to make to become a systemic team coach. All of these shifts mean that we are able to bring greater and more sustainable value to the client systems that we work with. They are as follows:

- From seeing coaching challenges as one-to-one challenges, to coaching the team in its wider system
- From facilitating away-days to partnering with a team, systemically, over time
- From coaching individual leaders to coaching for collective leadership.

From coaching one-to-one to coaching the team in its context - John's Story

My commitment to thinking more systemically first in individual coaching and then with teams came when a CEO I was coaching was removed from his position during the period I was coaching him. This came as a huge shock and an awakening to the limitations of individual coaching.

My coachee was very experienced and dynamic; this was his last role before retiring, so he wanted to leave a legacy of change and innovation. The first mistake on my part was being highly impressed by his values, vision and capability. He was keen to reflect and learn on how to be more effective in leading the company into the 21st Century. As he was the boss and sponsor of the coaching contract I thought there was no-one else to consult in a three way engagement. He indicated in passing that there was an 'old fashioned' board chair that he was hoping would be replaced shortly.

He was a typical Heroic Leader: out in front leading and motivating a 'weak management team' and in retrospect I can see that my coaching supported him in this stance. With no real feedback from the system, we were functioning in a bubble completely shaped by my coachee's perspective on how he was performing and the impact he was having. This was my second mistake – not to be more demanding in getting feedback from the board and his team.

A tragic event then overtook him. He was diagnosed with early stage cancer and needed four months off work to have urgent treatment and to convalesce.

Of course our coaching ceased immediately – we didn't even have a closing session and I was not in touch with the organisation in the meantime.

Some five months later I got a call from him to ask if we could meet, I assumed to re-engage in our coaching, but instead it was to share and explore the termination of his contract and the Company's generous offer of early retirement. What had happened was that the Chair had taken over in his absence and undone all the changes the CEO, my coachee, had put in place. His team had never properly bought into his vision and change of direction so they were happy to return to the old ways. After the illness he had no fight left to start again and challenge what had happened, so he accepted the package.

I was devastated and spent a good deal of time in supervision looking at why and how I'd failed to see the bigger picture and challenge my coachee's perspective on how he was relating to his team and their stakeholders. I was totally focused on serving my coachee and not holding the whole organisation's interests at heart. I was 'Systems Blind' to quote Barry Oshry[1].

It was some years later, but with this experience very live in my mind, that I met up with Peter Hawkins who explained his new Five Disciplines model of Systemic Team Coaching® and the Six Lenses. I recognised instantly that here was a framework that would not have allowed my situation to occur.

As coaches that work predominantly one-to-one, we know that we can help a coachee make major shifts in their capacity. But what John's story illustrates is that by focusing purely on the person, in isolation from his context, coaches can be blind to the real needs and challenges of the client system and also the needs of the person whom they believe they are helping. We may be supporting a coachee in maintaining a position that is untenable if we were to look at the needs of the system overall.

If you currently work as a one-to-one coach, consider:

- What if you were able to enhance your impact not only by coaching individuals, but also by coaching the relationships between them?
- What if you were able to hold a mirror to unhelpful relationships and team dynamics as they are occurring in the room and provide your coachees with the awareness and opportunity to be different – in the 'touchpoint' moment?

---

1. Oshry, Barry, Seeing Systems: *Unlocking the Mysteries of Organizational Life*, Berrett-Koehler Publishers, 1995

- What if you could help the whole team – not just the team leader– see that the habitual behaviours that stop them from performing at their best are not merely a function of personality differences but a function of the demands of the wider system?

Organisations are in reality a complex network of relationships. It is through relationship that things get done and it is through the inadequacies in relationship that organisation value is limited. In Margaret Wheatley's words *'relationships form the prime source of value in an enterprise'.*[2] Therefore the more you can enable the organisation to create greater value from its connections; person-to-person, group-to-group, unit-to-unit, the greater value you will bring.

By coaching the collective team, in a systemic way, we enhance their collective value, and are more impactful as coaches.

From facilitating away-days to partnering with a team, systemically, over time.

If you are experienced in team facilitation and team building, consider the following questions:

- How often are you called in to facilitate an away-day – maybe with Lens Four, to review a strategy, to help a team to get its annual morale boost; or with Lens Three, to help people to get to know each other better?

- How often do you know that the team leader's hopes for the day far exceed what can be achieved in that short space of time? Furthermore, you feel the need to 'fix' an impossible situation?

- How often do you find that the sense of excitement and good intent doesn't last far beyond the following week?

- How often do you secure agreement to a follow up session which reignites the good intentions but quickly fades away?

We are sure that these questions will have stimulated some familiar experiences for you. They are familiar to us too. But why sign up for these events when we know from experience that they only have a short-term impact? We wouldn't sign up for a one-off one to one coaching session, so why do it for a team when we are aware that the follow-through is going to be limited?

2. Wheatley, Margaret, *Leadership and the New Science: Discovering Order in a Chaotic World,* Berrett-Koehler, 1992

We know that sometimes the sponsor is only willing to finance an initial workshop (as in the example of the six lenses in Chapter 1). They will only sign up for the next step after they've taken the first one.

Many team leaders don't want to invest the time or money from their budget because they're not convinced of the value or are scared that it will show them up as inadequate. In addition, it's not uncommon to find team leaders who call in a team coach to help 'fix' a problem, hopefully in one step, rather than viewing them as an essential partner for a well-functioning team: someone whose contribution can only be fully realised by working together for a period of time.

So, one of our aims in writing this book and promoting the Systemic Team Coaching® approach is to educate and encourage team coaches and team leaders to use team coaching to move to a level of higher performance that can be sustained over time, rather than to address purely short term challenges and issues.

Even when our work with a team starts with a workshop or one-off intervention, it is critical as team coaches that we are aware of, and educate the client in the shortcomings of such an intervention. Our goal is always to help the client see that bringing real value to the team can only occur through a sustained partnering relationship between the coach and the team over time. This relationship is one of mutual trust, where change happens through experimentation, reinforcement of new ways of working and learning transfer.

In this partnership we move from working with the team and its internal dynamic to working with the team in context. As the story of the six lenses illustrates, this partnership does not only look at internal team dynamics. As coaches, our role goes far beyond facilitating meetings about personality types and how they can relate better to each other. As systemic team coaches we work with the team in context so we attend to the needs of the outside world on the team and the team's impact outwards, coaching the connections between the team and its key stakeholders.[3]

As a result the team coach can work as a true partner and witness the value of their endeavour in transformed performance of the team, not just a 'high' feeling at the end of a one-off away-day.

---

3. For in-depth discussion of the nature and value of partnership in the systemic team coach-client relationship, see Peter Hawkins, *Leadership Team Coaching*, Kogan Page 2017

From coaching leaders to coaching for greater collective leadership

Many leadership programmes draw leaders from across the business. They have great insights, and apply new skills with people they rarely work with. Then they go back to their teams and find it far more difficult than they expected to put the skills they learned and applied in the development programme into action with their day to day colleagues.

By contrast, the focus of the Systemic Team Coaching® approach is to develop leadership together: to help the team leader build individual capacity while also fostering a new collective leadership mentality in the team as a whole.

Critical to this is your stance as a systemic team coach, which must be one of partnering with the team leader and the team together. Care must be taken not to usurp the role of the team leader, as can happen when the coach takes control of the process or provides strong facilitation. You are coaching the team with its leader on the relationships that enable optimum collective leadership to be developed. (We develop this further in Chapter 6 on Leadership)

A key implication of this is that you have to broaden your concept of who it is you call the client. In Systemic Team Coaching® our client is not one individual leader, nor the team, but the business as a whole, in the context of its stakeholders and their needs, now and into the future and the implications of these for the purpose and work of the team.

Why would a team leader be interested in Systemic Team Coaching®?

Leaders have a complex range of issues to consider at the same time – demands from customers, shareholders, the board, the team and the wider organisation. As executive coaches we can help our leader-coachees to develop new strategies, approaches and leadership capacity for addressing and making sense of this complexity, as illustrated in John's story at the beginning of this chapter.

How, then, can we convince a leader that working with a systemic team coach can unlock even greater value for them and their business?

Here are some of the points that we use when talking to a team leader:

A systemic team coach:

1. Brings a fresh set of eyes to relationships and connections between you, the team and its stakeholders. This helps you as a leader to stand back, gain a new perspective on the reality of your team meetings, your interactions with the wider organisation and the factors impeding your performance.

2. Holds up a mirror to your leadership in action – with your team in the moment – and helps you see where you add value now and where your current behaviour and responses impede the best use of your team's skills and contributions.

3. Brings awareness to the collective dynamic of the team, providing coaching not only to individual team members but to the relationships between them. This helps to bring the unconscious and unspoken patterns, assumptions and behaviours into the conscious awareness of the team and its stakeholders.

4. Partners with you and your team over time.

5. Represents a lower investment cost than coaching each team member and the impact is greater, because the team relationships are transformed in action.

In our experience, if the team leader is open to developing their leadership capacity and can feel that we're behind them in doing that live with their team, then the leader and the team will make remarkable strides forward in performance.

Why would a team be interested in Systemic Team Coaching®?

The Five Disciplines framework is designed to foster high performance in teams. If a team leader is willing and able to learn and guide the team to attend to each discipline then the team can progress effectively without a coach. (AoEC have also developed a Systemic Team Leadership programme which provides team leaders with the same Five Disciplines framework focused on their using it themselves with their teams.)

If the team can see the value of systemic thinking and application, then having a systemic team coach will guide and focus it on its blind spots and challenge and support the members to face difficult choices and actions.

Some questions that we ask a team to help them start exploring the value of Systemic Team Coaching:®

- How far are you aware of the value you get from the meetings you hold with your team?

- What's different between the value you get from coming together and speaking to your colleagues one to one?

- How long after the high of a successful away-day are you able to witness the value of the investment of time and money?

- How often do you agree a set of actions only later to find that things are not progressing as you expected?

- If you to stand back from your business, where are the places where projects stall? Where is communication blocked? Where do people or groups persistently fail to rise to their potential? How often do you or others blame the issue on personalities? Or interpersonal conflicts?

As you'll see later in the book when we talk about the Systemic Team Coaching® Process, by expanding these questions into a diagnostic enquiry process, especially using our Team Connect 360 survey, we can engage the team in identifying how it can 'raise its game' and collectively become more effective.

Summary.

- Systemic Team Coaching® brings greater value to the organisation compared to individual one-to-one coaching by attending to stakeholder requirements and impact.

- Coaching the team over time rather than the one-off team development workshop helps build a sustained change in behaviour and performance.

- When we move from coaching the team leader to coaching the team, we can help build collective leadership and ownership for the achievement of the team's objectives and targets.

- There are different ways to engage a team leader and a team in conversations about the value of the Systemic Team Coaching®approach.

3

THE FIVE
DISCIPLINES
FRAMEWORK

Questions covered in this chapter

- What are the Five Disciplines for successful team working?
- How do the Five Disciplines connect to create this framework?
- What is the systemic team coach's role in each of the disciplines?
- What are the questions in the Team Connect 360 survey tool for each discipline?

Coaching the five disciplines of successful team practice

This elegant and highly practical framework was created by Peter Hawkins and is described in detail in both his books *Leadership Team Coaching*[1] and *Leadership Team Coaching in Practice*[2].

The framework has been developed into a diagnostic survey: Team Connect 360 which facilitates the team in

- Evaluating how it currently functions
- Understanding how current practice may be contributing to or hindering performance
- Providing the team with guidance on how and where to develop its effectiveness.

The framework has two dimensions: Inside/Outside the team and Task/People functions combined to produce a four-box model (Fig. 3.1, below). By looking at the outside of the team as an integral part of the team's work, Peter has cemented the importance of a systemic perspective in the team's functioning.

Fig. 3.1: Four-box Model

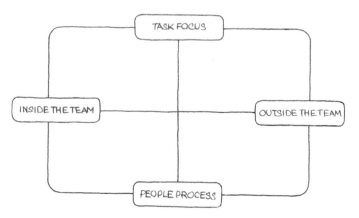

1. Hawkins, P, *Leadership Team Coaching*, Kogan Page, 2014
2. Hawkins, P, (Ed) *Leadership Team Coaching in Practice*, Kogan Page 2014

The first dimension raises a critical question that we always address when working with a new team:

Who is *inside* the team and who is closely connected but *outside* the team?

Those *inside* the team are a small number of people with complementary skills who are committed to a common purpose, set of performance goals and approach for which they hold themselves mutually accountable.[3]

Those *outside* the team are classed as stakeholders: they have an investment in the team's performance and outcomes but are not involved in the delivery of the outcomes.

This is not always a straightforward question, as many teams have temporary or occasional members or ones with multiple roles e.g. a family firm where the owner is on the board, on the executive team and also heads up the sales team. So she would be inside three teams and a stakeholder to the other two – glorious complications!

One of the first exercises we tend to use to clarify this question is to help the team draw up a Stakeholder Map (see Fig. 3.2, below). We write the team in the middle of the page and then ask the team members to identify and arrange the stakeholders around it according to the importance of each, and the quality of the team's relationship with each individual or group. You can do this with post it notes or objects, depending on how creative you want to be. We have mentioned the importance of the stakeholder interface earlier in this book (lens five of the six lenses of the Systemic Team Coaching® approach), and this is where we'd start to identify what that looks like.

Fig. 3.2: Diagram of a Stakeholder Map

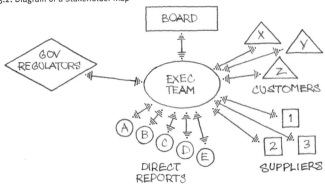

3. Katzenbach and Smith, Harvard Business Review, March 1993

The other dimension in the Five Disciplines Model has two elements:

- **Task Focus:** addressing the purpose, vision, strategy, delivery of objectives, systems and roles, etc. – all the more cognitive 'what and why' of running a business or community.

- **People Process:** interpersonal relationships, team dynamics, leadership style, culture, values, etc. - all the more emotional 'who and how' aspects.

When we combine these two dimensions we arrive at four boxes, or disciplines of a team, which Hawkins has entitled:

- **Commissioning – Stakeholder Expectations**
- **Clarifying – Team Tasks**
- **Co-Creating – Team Relationships**
- **Connecting – Stakeholder Relationships**

There is also a fifth discipline in the centre – but we will come to this later.

Fig. 3.3

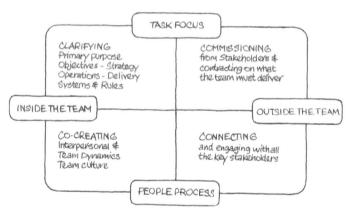

It is important to be clear that these are the disciplines that we expect the team to be performing well if it is to be effective. It is NOT a set of steps in the Systemic Team Coaching® process. The role of the systemic team coach is to help the team to

- Be aware of its performance in each of these disciplines
- Understand the impact of each discipline on overall team performance
- Enhance its effectiveness in each discipline.

While Hawkins orders the disciplines from one to five, as described below, the systemic team coach needs to help the team identify and decide which discipline to attend to first in the service of team performance improvement.

We now look at each discipline in turn, the systemic team coach's role in it and how the online Team Connect 360 tool enquires into this discipline.

Discipline 1: Commissioning - Stakeholder Expectations

The first discipline focuses on what the stakeholders expect of the team. For a team to be successful in meeting the business objectives it needs clear directives on what is required from the stakeholders it serves. This includes a clear purpose and defined success criteria by which the performance of the team will be assessed.

It will be for the primary stakeholder (the individual/team/group that the team reports into) to define the primary commission and for the team to negotiate the final terms. Too often a team proceeds without an explicit and clear directive on what it is required to deliver and sets about doing what it thinks is best, only to be criticised later in the year for under-achievement. Furthermore the commission should be up for quarterly review so a 'recommission' can be negotiated if circumstances change.

In addition, there will be other stakeholders (peers, teams, reports, clients, customers and suppliers) who will have an influence on how the team is expected to perform and the way it's success will be measured. The team has to be aware of competing demands from different stakeholders and find a way of creating a climate of dialogue between them so that they are constantly in touch with what is needed from them.

A clear commission is not only a function of a clear statement or dialogue about what the commissioners require of the team. It also needs to be backed up by the resources of money, time and room for manoeuvre needed by the team to fulfil the agreed purpose. We have worked with teams where the statement of requirement from the board to a leadership team was clear, but the behaviour of board members showed clearly that they did not trust or support the team to deliver what was required. Team progress was therefore impossible without further constructive dialogue between the team and its board about the need for the intent to be translated into clear sponsorship. (This is illustrated in Chapter 4: Co-missioning, *Leadership Team Coaching in Practice*)[4]

4. Hilary Lines, in Hawkins,P. (Ed), *Leadership Team Coaching in Practice*, Kogan Page 2014

The role of the systemic team coach

A key role of the systemic team coach in this discipline is to help the team engage robustly with its primary and other stakeholders, in order to help the team address the fundamental question: *What do our stakeholders, now and in the future, demand of us?* Addressing this question is essential if the team is to develop a clear view of its purpose in the wider system in which it sits. Part of the coach's role may be to help the team research and make new sense of stakeholder needs and views. It may also include coaching the team in the skills and techniques of dialogue and negotiation through which they can build more open and productive partnership with those stakeholders.

The systemic team coach can also be required to coach the relationship between the team and external stakeholders, such as the Chair (if this is an executive team) or CEO (if this is a senior management team). Or they may be required to extend their coaching to these more senior people. This can be a demanding intervention for the coach, who will be required to challenge the 'bosses' and coach them to be clearer in their expectations and potentially to face reality and compromise on what they want.

Team Connect 360 questionnaire asks the following questions in this discipline:

Does your team...

1. Have a clear understanding of the expectations of its different stakeholders?
2. Conduct reviews with its stakeholders to agree any changes in expectations?
3. Have a clear purpose based on the expectations of its different stakeholders?
4. Regularly spend time discussing and agreeing the scope of its activities based on the expectations of the stakeholders?
5. Display genuine commitment to the overall purpose and what it needs to deliver for its stakeholders?

Example

We were working with a senior marketing team who had been asked by their CEO to come up with some new strategies for building the business. The team took a day out of their normal work to brainstorm and develop some proposals for the long-term development of the business. They proudly invited the CEO to look at their proposals. His response was a surprise to them. 'I didn't want ideas for the long term,' he said, 'I wanted ideas for the next two months up to year-end'. The team was shocked – how could they have got this so wrong? What could the team have done to better and fully understand the CEO's needs before they invested time in all that unnecessary work?

The CEO's response also provoked a deeper questioning about the team's role and their relationship with their primary stakeholder: did he think that their only role was to develop short-term solutions? Did he expect them to have a voice in long-term strategy? If not, what needed to shift in their relationship with him to convince him that this was a legitimate – and value-creating – part of their purpose and role in the business? With the coach's help, they started to plan to have a different type of conversation with their CEO about what the Executive team needed of the Marketing team, and vice versa.

Discipline 2: Clarifying - Team Tasks

Having ascertained what the stakeholders require, the team then needs to jointly clarify and agree how it will execute this expectation. To be effective, the team members have to create a collective endeavour that is challenging for them to achieve. It has to be compelling and rewarding for both the team as a whole and each individual member. This must be an endeavour that can only be achieved by all members working together.

This involves addressing:

1. Purpose or Shared Endeavour

2. Vision

3. Strategy

4. Objectives/Targets

5. Systems, Processes & Protocols

6. Roles & Responsibilities

7. Values

1. Purpose or Shared Endeavour

This first area of focus requires the team to explore and agree the most fundamental question: What are we here to do together? For many teams this question can seem too obvious to ask, but avoid asking it at your peril! We frequently encounter teams where the individual views of the team's purpose vary far more widely than the team leader would have guessed. One powerful way of finding out is to ask each team member, without discussion, to write down their answers to the following question:

What can this team uniquely provide that our stakeholders need, now and in the future?

Then ask the team members to share their answers and explore the differences between them.

Exploring the team purpose is a critical way to unearth the motivation and energy of individual members, surface differences of opinion and renew a sense of passion and commitment within the team, as a foundation for a new strategy or plan.

The role of the systemic team coach

Our objective here is to help the team achieve the alignment and shared commitment that will drive energy and performance. The challenge for the coach is that differences in perspective are often subtle and intangible. We need to be tuned in to differences in perspective, ambition and language, and to drive for common understanding where differences arise, however seemingly slight. As you help the team build a common statement from the different responses to the question above, be sure to leave enough time, because you – and they – will be surprised at the differences that will emerge!

The systemic team coach also plays a vital role in encouraging the team to see its purpose in the context both of:

- Its external stakeholders (the outside-in perspective) and
- The needs of future stakeholders (the future-back perspective).[5]

The team's stated purpose is not just an amalgamation of the goals of its team members, but the product of the team's role in relationship with those bodies that it serves, both now and in the future. So it needs to be developed in the context of its work with its commissioning bodies and in the knowledge of their hopes, needs and aspirations for the work of the team.

2. Vision

This is the process of the team exploring together what the future will look like if it is successful in its shared endeavour. This is often not easy since in many cases the complexity of the world makes it hard to imagine. However, the process of 'stepping into a future place' and defining what will be different if the product of the team's work is a success, provides an important opportunity to raise team aspiration, clarify individual hopes and define the future in terms of outcomes.

5. Hawkins, P, *Leadership Team Coaching*, Kogan Page, 2014

The role of the systemic team coach

Here, too, a 'future-back and outside-in' perspective is vital, so the coach needs to create exercises that help the team to draw in the stakeholder voice.There are a wide range of tools and techniques here, from time-lines, to creating collages, pictures, news stories, documentaries and so on. Whatever you choose to use, through challenging and supportive facilitation, you can help the team develop a vision for the future that:

- Reflects stakeholder expectations and needs, now and in the future
- Is more compelling and inspiring than anything that could have been developed alone
- Draws on the diverse aspirations and perspectives of all team members.

3. Strategy

This is the high level plan for delivering the Vision and Mission/Purpose – the broad thinking that will give shape to the specific objectives and targets. Often the team leader will take it on herself to fashion this initial plan and, while this is expedient, it deprives the team of taking part in grappling with the What and How of achieving the vision.

The role of the systemic team coach

To facilitate the whole team as part of this strategic planning and therefore having full buy-in to fulfilling it or changing it if circumstances demand.

4. Objectives and Targets

This is getting down to what, specifically, the team is going to deliver and when.

The role of the systemic team coach

There is a whole raft of expertise around project planning that the coach may not know about. He should be asking precisely how the implementation is going to happen at this level. It may be that an expert is brought in to offer expertise in this arena. The work here sets the measures that will identify if the team are successful.

5. Systems, Processes and Protocols

The challenge now is HOW the team is going to deliver all of the above. Does the team have the necessary systems and processes in place? If not, what is the team going to do about it? The team may have a great vision, great strategy and well-defined targets but not the resources to deliver it, so facilitating this discussion will be of utmost importance.

In specific situations, technical solutions may be brought in or imposed eg. Change Management Processes, Total Quality or Lean Six Sigma.

The role of the systemic team coach

To help the team examine the systems and processes they currently have in place and how they go about using them as a team. This may result in surfacing habitual and safe routines then challenging the team to find more efficient or new ways of delivering the stated objectives.

6. Roles and Responsibilities

Who does what? This begins to link into the third Discipline: Co-creating, which focuses on people processes. Essentially it is about ensuring that the set objectives and the processes required to achieve them have team members allocated who are capable and responsible for following through, and most importantly, that the team identifies where they can act independently and where they need to act interdependently for the team to achieve more than the sum of its parts.

The role of the systemic team coach

To ensure that individual team members are clear on what their personal responsibility is to the team's objectives, over and above their function role and responsibility, and what they need from each other to serve the team in the best way. It's important to ensure any difficulties and ambiguities are surfaced, discussed and resolved. It is often the case that the tensions that are identified as personality clashes actually result from lack of clarity in roles and accountabilities.

A key aspect of this work for an executive team is to explore what the key strategic areas are that the team shares accountability for, and how these will be led and managed within the team. Addressing this is important if the team is to develop its collective leadership – a topic we return to in Chapter 6.

7. Values

This is about helping the team to explore and agree what guiding principles, values and codes of behaviour underpin their purpose and their work together. It helps the team to be explicit about the unspoken reasons and principles that will underpin its decision-making and behaviour, and forms the basis for its behaviour within the team and its leadership within the wider world. It is important that team values are fully owned by the members and are created from deep level conversations about what really matters to each person in their work with this team and this organisation.

The role of the systemic team coach

To encourage a team to spend time on this area since it provides an important foundation on which the collective leadership of the team can be built. Some teams may find this area too 'fluffy' or may take for granted that values exist and are lived by, without explicitly exploring whether this is really the case.

As the importance of values-based or ethical leadership is recognised, the systemic team coach plays a key role in holding the team accountable for exploring the way it interacts with the world, the ethical basis for its practices and the legacy it is leaving in the world.

Meaningful discussions of values can open up sensitive and personal areas of disclosure for team members. The systemic team coach needs to create a safe and contained space that engenders respect for difference, and enables candid conversation to take place.

Team Connect 360 questionnaire asks the following questions in this discipline:

Does your team...

- Have a clear and agreed sense of its purpose?
- Have a well-developed strategy?
- Have clear objectives and collective team Key Performance Indicators?
- Put in place the practical systems and processes to deliver its strategy?
- Operate with clear individual and team roles and responsibilities?

Discipline 3: Co-creating - Team Relationships

Co-creating focuses on how to achieve more as a combined unit rather than as separate individuals through the interpersonal aspects of the team's work.

In order to deliver the joint endeavour, the team needs to work together, productively managing their collective capacities and limitations. The aim of the team must be to gain optimum value from the diverse capacities, skills and styles of its members. There are many assessment tools available to do this.

The effective team also builds trust in each other so it is able to harness diverse perspectives to make constructive, informed decisions. This discipline also focuses on how creative, innovative and adaptive the team can be in order to meet the demands of primary and other stakeholders.

While most teams have a designated leader who has overall responsibility for the team management and performance, Systemic Team Coaching® encourages the team to develop collective or devolved leadership. This means that the strengths and expertise of individual members are drawn to the fore when necessary and their leadership in this area at this time is acknowledged. It also means that the co-creating discipline needs to look at the relationship dynamic between team and team leader and how this needs to be developed to encourage greater shared leadership. We look at this more in Chapter 6.

The role of the systemic team coach

The co-creating discipline is often the one that is most familiar to team coaches, and the one they are frequently asked by team leaders to work on. This is traditional team facilitation and is often associated with 'teambuilding'. It requires the systemic team coach to understand group dynamics and interpersonal behaviour. Many psychologically-based team coaches will rely on psychometric instruments to identify individual personality preferences (e.g., MBTI, Firo-B, Insights) and role preferences (Belbin, Team Management Systems) and to help the team explore the impact of such preferences on interpersonal relationships, team dynamics and how work gets done. Others take an 'action oriented' approach: team games, outdoor challenges, interpersonal exercises will rely on experiential activities to diagnose team engagement from observation and analysis.

At AoEC we draw heavily from the principles of Gestalt coaching,[6] where we help the team to slow down in its work and enhance its awareness of how it is behaving and relating, in order to help it to be most resourceful in attending to its unhelpful patterns and turning up its more helpful ones.

But if we are to work systemically, we need to hone our skill as coaches in seeing where relationship issues in the room are a function of external systemic patterns, a phenomenon known in psychodynamics as 'parallel process'. This is the area of expertise that most coaches need to pay attention if they are to work systemically with teams. We explore this aspect of the Systemic Team Coaching® toolkit later in this book.

6. John Leary-Joyce, *The Fertile Void, Gestalt Coaching at Work*, AoEC Press, 2014

Team Connect 360 questionnaire asks the following questions in this discipline:

Does your team...

- Draw on the right mix of people and skills to achieve its goals?
- Actively engage its members, who leave meetings feeling more aligned, focused and motivated?
- Encourage different members to take on leadership of the team when appropriate?
- Manage differences constructively to resolve any conflict?
- Engage the talents and energies of all team members to generate new thinking and innovative ideas?
- Encourage members to hold each other accountable for their commitment to the team objectives?

Discipline 4: Connecting - Stakeholder Relationships

The team must now connect outside itself to engage staff and stakeholders to develop the type of relationships that will drive improvements in the team's and organisation's performance. This involves being tuned in to the organisational culture and how it evolves as well as being aligned with the wider Political, Economic, Social, Technological, Legal and Environmental (PESTLE) context.

Managing these relationships is the responsibility of the whole team and not just the team leader. The team needs to present a unified front to all stakeholders, while adapting the message to fit the requirements of different stakeholder groups. For example, the style of communication with staff members would need to be different from the communication styles used with customers or with shareholders.

The role of the systemic team coach

The systemic team coach needs to ensure that the team is aware of all the stakeholders and how they manage the various stakeholder relationships. Often one stakeholder will be minimised or forgotten which can result in political or cultural difficulties later on. She also has to make sure that the voice of all stakeholders is heard in the team and difficult dynamics are surfaced and addressed.

Often in this discipline the systemic team coach's role is to help the team to improve and develop the way that it turns its intentions into actions. Our work may include challenging the team to voice out loud how it will communicate its strategy and plan, through the use of 'fast-forward role plays', inviting other team members to sit in the chair of each of the key stakeholders, listen to each other's communication and to give feedback on the content and style of the message conveyed.

Team Connect 360 questionnaire asks the following questions in this discipline:

Does your team...

- Communicate effectively with each of its stakeholders to engage and influence?

- Display a real insight into the needs of the organisation and what is important to each stakeholder?

- Seek feedback from its different stakeholder groups at appropriate intervals?

- Distribute responsibility for their stakeholder relationships amongst its members?

- Ensure that each team member represents the whole team when engaging with its stakeholders?

Discipline 5 - Core Learning

Fig. 3.4: The 5th Discipline - Core Learning

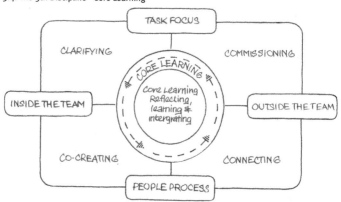

At the centre of the model in the diagram above (Fig. 3.4) is the Core Learning Discipline: where the team stands back and reflects on its own performance, to consolidate the learning from the successes achieved and the mistakes it has overcome and to explore how it can use these experiences to enhance its performance in the future.

To fulfil this discipline the team pays attention to what they're doing in each of the four preceding disciplines and to identify where they are working well and where they need to focus more effort and energy to achieve better results. This means inviting feedback from stakeholders and encouraging honest conversations internally, between themselves.

The role of the systemic team coach

Teams can to easily be caught up in the whirlwind of achieving targets and future plans that they forget (at best) or neglect to reflect on and review the learning from past performance. The task of the systemic team coach here is to remind the team that this reflection is a valuable activity, building the sustainability and resilience of the team. It tends to work best if included in the regular debrief discussions in any discipline rather than as an event in itself. However, re-running a Team Connect 360 survey is a good way to review the core learning of the team annually. Reviewing the achievements and development of the team against its original objectives for the team coaching is also vital.

Helping the team to learn and to be aware of its learning is crucial to enable the team to build its self-sufficiency after the coach's work is complete.

Team Connect 360 questionnaire asks the following questions in this discipline:

Does your team...

- Generate individual and team learning from its successes and failures on a regular basis?
- Conduct regular reviews to explore what is and isn't working for the team and for its stakeholder relationships?
- Find creative solutions to adapt quickly to change?
- Use regular feedback, challenge and support from within and outside the team to support collective development?
- Use the leaving and joining of team members as a learning experience?

Summary

The five disciplines framework is a foundational model for the systemic team coach, that:

- Helps the team attend to the important external aspects as well as the internal perspectives of the team's work

- Provides a map and a diagnostic tool against which the work of the team can be designed and the performance of the team reviewed and measured

- Serves as guidance for team coaching interventions. For example, a full workshop can be designed around the following steps:

  - What do we want to learn?

  - What do our stakeholders need and want from us?

  - What do we collectively commit to do?

  - How do we need to work with each other?

  - How will we take our actions away and engage differently with stakeholders?

  - What have we learnt?

4

THE SYSTEMIC TEAM COACHING® PROCESS

Questions covered in this chapter

- When does the Systemic Team Coaching® process start?
- How do we best inquire into the system?
- Who do we involve, and how?
- What is the place of the team leader?
- When and how do we contract? And for what?
- How do we decide *where* to start?
- How do we create a partnership through our coaching work?

In this chapter we describe the process that we use to conduct a Systemic Team Coaching® programme, from the point of first contact with the client system to the closure of the work.

Peter Hawkins in Leadership Team Coaching[1] presents this process flow in 6 phases as CIDCLEAR:

- **Contract**
- **Inquire**
- **Diagnosis**
- **Contract**
- **Listen, Explore, Act**
- **Review**

The repetition of 'Contracting' in this CIDCLEAR model illustrates the importance of multiple contracting throughout the process of the team coaching work, starting with agreeing the contract necessary to commence the inquiry work, and later contracting to engage the whole team in the process of coaching. The inclusion of the CLEAR coaching cycle in the model underlines the centrality of coaching – rather than consulting or facilitation – to the work of the systemic team coaching. The process is one of continually judging when to re-contract, listening to what is being said and left unsaid, exploring more broadly and deeply to create more awareness and understanding, encouraging new thought and action and reviewing and learning from each cycle.

Drawing on the principles of CIDCLEAR, we set out below a variation on that model – The Systemic Team Coaching® Five Phase Process: SIDER which, we believe, more clearly articulates the spirit of working systemically and in partnership with the client.

Phase 1: Scoping and building relationships and agreement with Sponsor and Team Leader

Phase 2: Inquiry into the team and its context

Phase 3: Developing the team coaching agenda, collaboratively with team leader and team; contracting for the work

Phase4: Execution and Engagement – coaching to fulfil the development agenda

1. Peter Hawkins, *Leadership Team Coaching*, Kogan Page 2017 pp 81-99

Phase 5: Review, Evaluation and Learning

We encourage all our students to develop their own process models. The titles we use are less important than the creation of a road map against which we can plan our work, orient and re-orient ourselves in the midst of the programme, and provide the sense of journey, informed by experience, to the client team and sponsor.

Below we describe the process that we use under the five phases of the Systemic Team Coaching® process.

Phase 1. Scoping, Relationship Building and Agreement with the Sponsor and Team Leader

The Systemic Team Coaching® process usually starts with an invitation from the sponsor – a person who has identified a learning need for a team and has taken responsibility for initiating the engagement with you. The sponsor may be the team leader, the team's boss or an HR professional. This person usually controls the budget with the ability to sign off the work so will have some investment in the successful outcome of the Systemic Team Coaching®.

Team Leader as Sponsor – on one level this makes the next Inquiry phase easier since the sponsor will have a real commitment to the team development, good knowledge of the team members, key stakeholders and general context for the work. He will generally be able to give you a sound and extensive briefing on the situation and what outcomes he wants. The downside is that you will have to make more effort and probably challenge to get access to the primary stakeholder, the team leader's boss, because the team leader may be reticent in getting his boss involved in case she 'interferes' to much.

Team's Boss as Sponsor – this would be the primary stakeholder (not the team leader) who sets the commission for the team so has a big investment in the outcome. Having the senior leader engaged is a big advantage from the perspective of support and commitment to the Systemic Team Coaching® process. The downside is that she will know the team from the outside and may find it easier to 'blame' the team for underperforming and not want to see her own part in the problems involved. In this case there may be a level of imposition of the intervention on the team which will require more time to ensure full commitment from the team and team leader.

Third Party (Head of Coaching, OD Professional, HR Business Partner) as Sponsor – in this case the 'third party sponsor' will have identified a difficulty in the team and will usually have discussed the potential solution with the team leader. She is more likely to have researched the Systemic Team Coaching® approach and chosen it from others so she will probably have prepared the ground for you in advance with the team leader and his boss. The downside is that she is unlikely to know the team well and her understanding of the situation will be from the outside: third hand. She may only have a connection with the team through the leader so further limitation to really understanding what the key issues are.

After the initial connection to discuss the potential work, there is generally a first meeting with the sponsor and the team leader (if different) to outline the scope of the work. You may feel it's useful at this stage to explain the Systemic Team Coaching® process and your approach to the 5 Disciplines model, so you set the tone and parameters. This will give the client a sense of how you work and what you think it is important to consider in a team coaching programme, what outcomes can be expected and the possible timeframe. Usually there will be a discussion on costs, fees, and budget/time constraints.

If you are an executive coach or consultant you will be familiar with this process and have your own way of conducting these initial meetings. If you are an internal coach or consultant it is equally important that you set out clearly how you work, what timeframe and budget will be required and the commitments and working relationships needed to make this type of programme successful.

There may well be a bidding process for the work, through which the sponsor will assess your appropriateness for the team and explore aspects of 'chemistry'. It is important to note that, as in one-to-one coaching, it is vital that any judgment about 'chemistry' is two-way: you need to be happy that you can work with the team, as well as the other way round.

We consider it vital that you meet the team leader separately (if he is not the sponsor) to be sure that he is:

- Prepared to be fully engaged in the coaching work
- Willing, as part of the team coaching, to look at his own leadership and its impact on team effectiveness

- Prepared to allow you to engage in a process of Inquiry so that you fully understand the perspectives of team members and stakeholders on the current team's functioning and what it wants to change
- Able to take challenge from you and to learn
- Someone with whom you can work.

If this cannot be confirmed, an alternative to team coaching may be a better choice for this team.

Paying attention to first impressions: 'tuning in' to the client's system and its leadership, and agreeing the Inquiry

When we visit a country for the first time, we are immediately struck by its difference from our familiar environment: we notice unfamiliar things. We may have to think consciously about how to do certain things as our habitual expectations and habits are challenged. Gradually, as we spend time in this new environment, and later as we revisit the place, the things that seemed so unusual on our first visit become more familiar and fade into the background. We accept them as normal.

So it is with organisational systems that we encounter, but only if we are awake and alert to what the system can tell us at our early encounters with it, which is why we use the term 'tuning in'. You need to pay attention to aspects of behaviour, relationship, language and dynamic that can tell you something about that it is like to work there. This is important data, that can provide contextual meaning to your later work with the team.

Questions to consider

Consider receiving a phone call from a company Chair asking you to coach her CEO, and hearing the impatience and irritation in the Chair's voice. What might this tell you about the relationship between the Chair and the CEO and its place in the coaching assignment? What might it tell you about the pressures on the board? What will you be curious about?

Consider attending a first team meeting and being struck with a sense of anxiety and tension in your chest. What might this tell you about the environment which you have just entered? Imagine that your anxiety might be impacted by a frantic sense of pace and urgency in the working environment. What might this mean for how you manage yourself in working with this system? What do syou stay alert to?

Consider going to talk to a new team about the work they want you to do and the team leader is absent. What might this say about their relationship with the team and their expectations of you and your future work with the team? What might you need to do or say early in the coaching work?

Of course there can be many reasons for the above phenomena but the important point is that these early observations are key data for the systemic team coach. This means that the coach needs to be open to this data, using what we call 'undirected awareness'; he needs to log it and allow it to feed his curiosity about the system he is entering, while resisting from judging it.[2,3] We will talk about how to do this in the next section.

Preparing for Phase 2: The Inquiry

Agreeing to proceed with the work will involve agreeing the initial scope of the work with the team leader, sponsor (if different) and the team. This will include:

- Agreeing a process by which you will get to know the views and needs of individual members
- Agreeing how feedback data will be collected from team stakeholders
- Initial agreement on what involvement is required from the primary stakeholder for the coaching to be effective
- Meeting with the team as a whole to explain the nature and scope of Systemic Team Coaching®, how they will be involved and the commitment required from them to derive value from the process
- Reaching clarity about how inquiry data will be handled, in terms of boundaries of confidentiality between one-to-one and team conversations, data collected from individual stakeholders, who will receive the feedback first, and how the data will be shared with the team as a whole.

Essentially, this enables you to commence the Inquiry process, having ensured that the team knows what to expect and how they will be engaged.

---

2. To further explore the 'use of self' as an OD practitioner, look at Jonno Hanafin and Mary Anne Rainey Tolbert in *Use of Self in OD Consulting: What Matters is presence,* In NTL *Handbook of Organisational Development and Change,* 2006.

3. Also see Ed Nevis, *Organizational Consulting: A Gestalt Approach,* Gestalt Institute of Cleveland, 1997.

The knotty question of confidentiality

Immediately we start to engage with a client system, questions of confidentiality start to arise.

- When we are briefed by the team leader or sponsor, who else is privy to this information?
- How should we handle this?
- Who will have access to the one-to-one conversations data collected?
- How do we manage the boundaries between one-to-one coaching and team coaching?

We have encountered two main models for handling the boundary between one-to-one and team conversations:

The first is that the team coach commits to keeping all one-to-one conversations anonymous and confidential, but agrees to share broad themes with the team from the data collected. The team coach encourages team members to take responsibility for sharing with the team any data that they share confidentially where it will clearly benefit the team's performance. This approach is useful especially where there is nervousness about the team coaching intervention and a lack of trust within the team. It can help to build confidence early in the process.

The second model is that the team coach agrees with the team that all data and perspectives are shared – one-to-one or team conversations – as part of the team coaching work and therefore can be disclosed by the team coach within the team (not stakeholders). This has the advantage of:

- Focusing the one-to-one session on helping the team member explore team issues and his role in the team rather than private coaching matters separate from the team.
- Ensuring that the team coach is not carrying private and confidential information about the team that cannot be disclosed
- Emphasising that the 'client' is the team and the members are subsets of the team.The team coach inviting personal disclosure about the team in this manner may result in limited sharing. However it may be better for this 'secret' information to emerge in due course than to be left carrying it privately.

Whichever approach you adopt, it is important that you do not become the channel through which 'private' information is shared in the team. Rather, your role is to coach team members to share more freely themselves. Only as a last resort will the team coach take action and only if it is considered necessary for the development of the team.

Phase 2. Inquiry into the team and its context

This is the process of really discovering the underlying issues and dynamics of the team in its organisational context. This involves

- Meeting the team members individually (phone or face to face). This is the essential basis for starting the Inquiry.

- Meeting the team to create a Stakeholder Map to identify the primary stakeholder and other key stakeholders who have influence over, or are impacted by the team

- Engaging with these stakeholders through structured interviews and/or Team Connect 360 questionnaire.

- Getting access to any other information – customer/employee surveys, personal profiling data, Key Performance Indicators, organisational plans, strategies, values etc.

- Analysing the data to identify the key themes and creating a working hypothesis

- Meeting with the team to jointly interrogate the data to arrive at a joint diagnosis and development plan/agenda.

Through this intense process you:

- Form a full picture of the team in its systemic context and bring the team to see the issues that need to be addressed

- Ensure that each team member feels engaged and is consulted on the team's focus and direction

- Set the tone for stakeholder involvement throughout the Systemic Team Coaching® engagement.

What if the sponsor does not see the value and is reluctant to pay for the Inquiry?

It is vital that you present this Inquiry work as a key benefit for the team not just for you. By drawing on the different views of team members and asking them questions that help them look at the team in ways that they are unaccustomed to, the coach is:

- Bringing new eyes to the work of the team

- Pulling together a perspective of its current situation and ways of working that is likely not to be obvious to the leader, the team or stakeholders up till now

- Starting the process of coaching through creating new awareness among team members

- Helping to build interest and engagement in the team coaching process among team members, including those who may initially be reluctant to engage or unenthusiastic. If the team doesn't have a shared view of the challenges the team faces, they are unlikely to commit to the programme of work to address these challenges

- Building a picture that will enable a new type of conversation to take place within the team

- Giving stakeholders a voice and influence in the development of the team.

Inquiring with Stakeholders

Traditional team coaching will help the team to address its own needs, regardless of the demands of the people and groups it serves. By generating a Stakeholder Map you are asking the question, *'How does the team serve the current and future needs of its stakeholders?'*

The stakeholder inquiry will, as a minimum, include seeking the views of the:

- 'Primary stakeholder', this is the 'boss' or the person/people the team reports into (in an executive team this would be the Chair and members of the board)

- Direct Reports – key people and groups who report to the team

- Representatives of client/customer and supplier groups or divisions within the organisation, and potentially external to the organisation.

There are times when a team leader is reluctant to disturb the waters by engaging stakeholders in the team coaching process. There are a number of approaches you can take in this instance:

- Agree to see just the Chair or team's boss in the first instance and to engage other stakeholders at a later date, when the value of this Inquiry may be more apparent to the team leader

- Ask the team to draw existing data together from feedback and internal surveys

- Encourage the team itself to collect data, using a proforma and guidance.

This can have the benefit of helping to improve stakeholder relationships while gaining new insights, but it is important to provide coaching support to the team to ensure that they are able to collect this data in an inquiring and objective way and not disrupt the Inquiry by engaging in debate or becoming defensive. This is likely to mean that you need to do some coaching with the team first, and help them collect stakeholder data later on in the team coaching programme[4].

Inquiry methods

Undirected Inquiry

The term 'undirected inquiry' (as outlined above) refers to using our senses to gather data as we notice it; this requires us to be open to what we hear, see, feel, experience, and to 'gather' this as data which we will incorporate into our knowledge-bank of what the client system is like. While this activity may sound simple to do, it is far more difficult in practice. For in order to see the data as an indication of how this system is functioning, we need to suspend our natural ability to interpret or make judgement about what we see.

Consider this example:

I was at the early stages of a team coaching assignment with an international team, and had commenced the Inquiry phase. I had agreed to interview all team members face to face, and this required me to travel to three different countries in the three-week period. I had agreed with the team leader that I would use the data from the one-to-ones to inform my draft design of the team's first off site meeting, to be held in five weeks' time. For me, it was – and is – important to keep my mind open to the data that I am collecting, to ensure that I have as full a picture as possible before closing my mind into a predetermined conclusion about a client team and the system in which it resides.

Unfortunately, the timescale for my one-to-one interviews slipped because of air transport problems beyond my control and my client asked me to go in to see her for an interim meeting. When I said that I was not yet able to share my findings (I was less than half way through) or to give her a detailed meeting

4. Peter Hawkins, *Leadership Team Coaching*, PP 84-87

design, she became agitated and expressed anger at my delay and started to question whether I had the experience to do this work.

My knee-jerk emotional response was one of anger at being blamed and offended that my competence was being questioned. I undoubtedly started to judge her as a difficult woman who was being very unreasonable. When I stood back from this experience, however, and treated it as 'data', I became curious about how my experience in this system reflected that of others who worked within in it. Did people feel pressured to reach decisions quickly? Was there a fear of appearing incompetent?– or of not being on top of things? As I got to know the client system more, I realised that the answer to these questions was "yes". Looked at through the lens of 'data', I could see that this experience, rather than being an unwelcome interruption to my Inquiry, was an invaluable early insight into the client system that I was starting to coach.

Directed Inquiry

We use the term 'directed inquiry' for structured methods of inquiry that enable us to look at certain aspects of the team's functioning. These include:

- Interviews - one-to-one, semi-structured
- 360 feedback tools
- Observing teams at work and other organisational data.

Interviews

It is important that your interview questions enable you to gain information on the multiple levels of the system relevant to the team: Personal – interpersonal – team dynamics – team mission and tasks – stakeholders and wider system. Thus the Six Levels and Five Disciplines models provide invaluable frameworks against which a questionnaire can be designed.

See **Appendix iii** in the Resources section at the end of this book for a semi-structured questionnaire that has been designed with reference to the Five Disciplines framework.

Just as important as the content of the Inquiry questions is how you use these early sessions to build a relationship. This is your first chance to show that you are holding the boundaries of the work, within which trust can grow, creating a safe space to explore and experiment. Be clear about how the data that you are collecting will be handled by you, and also what you expect from the interviewee in terms of taking this data forward.

An example might be:

'I am collecting all the data from the interviews and will sort it into themes on a non-attributable basis. I will not be saying who said what. But I will share the key themes with the team leader, and then with the whole team when we all meet together. The purpose of sharing the themes will be for the team to explore, add and discuss their meaning to them and to use this to discuss how and where the team coaching needs to start, to the benefit of the team overall. I will expect and encourage you to be open with your views when we get to that discussion, as part of your role in helping the team be more aware of its process and develop a more effective way of working.'

Considerations for the interviews

Cover the ground of the interview as far as possible, but don't be too structured. It is important to flow with the energy of the conversation and to follow your curiosity, so that you deepen your awareness of the emotional and cultural undertones of the team and its system.

Expect to find some resistance to the team coaching process. Resistance is a natural part of change and it is likely that you will find people who are anxious, fearful, sceptical or even dead against the idea of bringing in someone to work with the team. Make sure your way of being and questioning encourages the sharing of concerns and treats these as legitimate and understandable.

Remember that this is coaching, and the relationship that you build with each team member early in the engagement will influence the nature and tone of the work that follows. Take an interest in each person you meet: start to get to know them, what they do, who they are, what are their hopes and fears for this work. Treat them like human beings, not data sources!!

Take time between each interview to review your notes and to ensure that they are complete, and also to take note of any other data that you have collected through your senses – your somatic response, your feelings, any nuances of language or style. Save these for when you are reviewing the data as a whole.

360 degree feedback tools

An effective way of gaining team and stakeholder feedback is the use of a team 360 degree feedback tool. There is a choice of these on the market but we would recommend one that assesses the team according to the Five Disciplines framework, since this way your data has a systemic perspective. The AoEC Team Connect 360 (see Appendix ii in the Resources section at the end of this book), was developed in 2015 to fulfil this purpose.

Team Connect 360 (TC360) is an on-line diagnostic tool which invites responses from six groups:

- Primary Stakeholder
- Team Members
- Direct Reports
- Three other Stakeholders – suppliers, customers, colleagues or partners.

The Questionnaire focuses on six areas – each of the Five Disciplines plus a summary section:

- **Stakeholder Expectations (Commissioning)** – what the team is required to deliver
- **Team Tasks (Clarifying)** – what the team does to meet those expectations
- **Team Relationships (Co-creating)** – the interpersonal and leadership dynamics
- **Stakeholder Relationships (Connecting)** – how the team connects with those it serves
- **Team Learning (Core Learning)** – how the team develops to meet future challenges
- **Overall Productivity** – summary of the team's capacity to deliver.

In each of the Five Discipline sections there are three questions that are filled in by all respondents. A further two questions are then answered only by the team members. This is because there are certain internal dynamics and processes that only the team will know about. See Chapter 3 for the specific questions. The questions each have a 1 – 5 rating scale for simple and quick evaluation. There is a space for comments on each section to provide a more personal and qualitative perspective.

The report provides the aggregated results in colour graphs, which makes it easy to see the results plus the detailed comments on each section.

The advantages of TC360 as an Inquiry tool are:

- It is quick and efficient to administer
- There is a time and cost saving compared to individual interviews
- It avoids personal bias by an interviewer and is therefore more likely to be viewed as objective 'data' from the system

- Providing quantifiable measures is often more familiar and acceptable to teams and organisations
- It enables the collection of feedback from a wider range of stakeholders than might be feasible from one-to-one interviews, and may be deemed simpler and easier by busy stakeholders
- The team coach has graphic data as well as commentary that makes it simpler to debrief
- The team coach can then choose to do selective one-to-one interviews with key personnel
- At the Review stage a repeat 360 can be delivered to measure results of the Systemic Team Coaching® process[5].

Additional elements for the Inquiry Phase

Feedback for the team leader

As we have indicated earlier in this book, the development journey of the team leader is integral to the development journey of the team as a whole. One of the early questions you will explore with the team leader is how she wants her own leadership to develop as part of this team coaching intervention. She may have undertaken a leadership questionnaire which you can draw on or you can include specific questions in your interviews on the role and effectiveness of the team leader. This feedback would then be given in a one-to-one including agreement on how you will partner with the leader to explore and address the development areas that arise.

Using psychometrics and team assessment tools

A further element that can be included is a self-reporting psychometric assessment of the individuals and the team. There are a number on the market to draw on. This will build the team's collective awareness of personality preferences and working styles. It is most useful when addressing the team's dynamics in the Co-Creating Discipline, so best identified during the Inquiry Phase but administered later on in the Development Phase[6].

---

5. Peter Hawkins, *Leadership Team Coaching*, p 97
6. Peter Hawkins, *Leadership Team Coaching*, pp 86-87

Observing the team at work

Another aspect of gathering data about the team is to observe it in carrying out its normal business-as-usual work. It will be valuable data if you can sit in and observe at least one of each of a team's business meetings – ideally an operational meeting and a more strategic one, where they both exist.

Other organisational data

Before you work with a team it is important to build a broad picture of both the organisational and the broader business environment in which it works.

- Ask to see team performance data, sales figures, staff surveys, and customer and client feedback
- Be curious about the history of the team, changes in structure, leadership and membership that will impact on it today
- Take a broader look at how the business is viewed in the market, its position relative to competitors, where relevant
- Check out any factors in the wider environment: Political, Economic, Social, Technological, Legal, Environmental (PESTLE) that are impacting or may impact on it performance in the future
- Add this data to your picture of the team and its systemic influences.

Phase 3. Developing the Team Coaching Agenda, and Contracting for the Work

There are two important steps in making sense of the data in order to build a development agenda that is owned and supported by the team:

Step 1: Standing back from the data. This involves your taking the data you've gathered and identifying the key themes. It is vital to leave space and time to do this, so that you can really stand back from your interview notes, 360 report, other reports and personal 'undirected observations' to pull out the six main messages that you have heard. Working with a co-coach is most valuable here, as you share your different perspectives, challenge each other's judgements and assumptions, look for evidence for your themes and sharpen your thinking.

Step 2: Collaborative discovery: This second step involves engaging the team in the exploration of the themes. This normally happens at the first team coaching meeting after the Inquiry. If you have a consulting or business background, you may be tempted to produce a pristine presentation setting out the themes that you have identified. However, this would not be Systemic Team Coaching® – where the purpose is to raise the collective awareness of the team so that they can have a new type of conversation that will help them to start working in a different way.

When planning your data sharing session, it is important to consider the team leader's perspective and needs. How will the data be received by her and how might this reaction play into her leadership and relationship with the team? So you need to make a decision if you should share the data with the team leader first, before engaging the team. The advantages would be to:

- Gain her perspective as to how the findings might land with the team

- Provide any feedback to the leader that has been collected from the inquiry

- Help the leader prepare what she will say about how her own leadership role and practice contributes to the current situation, and what she is learning from this process so far. This will help her model openness in the conversation to follow.

Contracting with the team to proceed with the Development Phase

Once you are with the whole team, it is vitally important that you pay close attention to contracting. It may be useful to recap on the contracting steps that have got you to this stage. You will have:

- Agreed with the team sponsor and leader to undertake the inquiry and how the data will be handled

- Informed and gained agreement from each team member individually, the team collectively and any stakeholders about how the data will be handled and your commitment to confidentiality and anonymity

- Explained the purpose of the Inquiry to team members and emphasise that it will only be valuable if they actively engage in making sense of the data and are prepared to own the views that they have shared in the interviews or reporting process

- Shared the main themes that you've identified with the team leader in advance of the meeting, discussed her views about how the data will land with the team and agreed how you will work together live in the room.

You will then facilitate a contracting session to identify what team members need from each other and from the team coach or coaches to get the best from the session. From your perspective, this should include preparedness to be open with views, to listen to different perspectives and to seek to understand.

Following that you need to actively engage the team in the data analysis. This could include:

- Writing out the data on sheets of paper or cards and asking the team to organise it into themes
- Having a loose set of themes posted around the room plus a set of anonymous quotes from interviews and feedback reports. Asking the team to refine the themes and align the quotes to the themes
- Use the TC 360 data to examine each Discipline in turn to highlight the key themes
- Asking the team to explore the data in pairs or threes and to pick out quotes and comments that:
  - Resonate with them
  - They are curious about
  - They are concerned about
  - Are missing from the data so far.

Facilitating an open discussion creates:

- A deeper openness and understanding in the team of the key issues it faces
- New awareness of the current state of the team – what the strengths are and what is holding it back
- Willingness to engage in work to enhance its operation
- A new feeling of trust among team members, both in the process and in you, that this work will be worthwhile and that they will be heard and respected.

This will enable you to discuss and agree a Development Agenda with the team that will cover:

- Where the coaching work will start
- What the team wants to achieve through the coaching
- How the coaching will take place
- The time and resources that will be dedicated to it.

The Development Agenda and contract which builds the partnership for the team coaching therefore needs to include:

- A statement of the business outcomes the team needs to achieve from the coaching
- A statement of what the team as a whole and its members need to learn
- How the team and team coach need to work together to enable these goals to be met
- What the team members need from each other.
- The logistics and behavioural foundations of the coaching process: duration of the coaching process, frequency of meetings and location, confidentiality, and commitment to be present.

It is important to remember that team coaching is a process of learning[7], through which the team members, the team and the team coach grows and learns. Agreeing learning goals at the outset is key to starting to embed the importance of a learning and inquiring mindset into the team coaching process.

The following example provides a small illustration of this spirit of partnership:

In the early stages of their relationship, the team leader (TL) met with the team coach:

TL: *How will I be able to convince my team that we need to spend time on this coaching?*

Coach: *Let's pick that up with the team.*

At the Development meeting with the team:

Coach: *I understand that the result that you want to achieve from this coaching is to increase your sales by 15% and your customer satisfaction by two points.*

Team: *Yes.*

Coach: *Great. How much time are you prepared to invest in this coaching to get that result?*

---

7. Peter Hawkins, *Leadership Team Coaching*, pp 81-99

Phase 4. Executing and Engaging to Fulfil the Development Agenda

As we move from the process of making sense of the Inquiry data and creating a Development Agenda to engage in the team coaching, the relationship between you and the team should start to shift from 'inquirer' to 'partner'. This shift is subtle. It can best be facilitated by asking the question:

'How can we work together in a coaching relationship to best enable you and your stakeholders to fulfil your vision and goals for the team, the business as whole and your current and future stakeholders?'

Systemic Team Coaching® is not a process by which a sequence of coaching interventions are 'done to' a team; it is a process where two parties – the team and the team coach – agree to work together in the interests of the current and future stakeholder groups whom the team serves. In this sense the team and team coach face the future together in striving for an outcome in which both have an interest.

Peter Hawkins[8] maps out a logical sequence of working round the first four disciplines outlined in Chapter 3 of this book. It makes sense to start by ensuring that the team is clear about its stakeholder expectations (Commissioning Discipline). In this way the team is able to work on how it will go about delivering to these requirements in the Team Tasks – Clarifying Discipline. This will then give rise to how the team is configured in terms of the capacity of the team members and the quality of the relationships. This is the work in the Team Relationships – Co-Creating Discipline. The final step in the sequence is making sure that the team is building strong Connections through Stakeholder Relationships. Team Learning should be included in every event to embed a habitual process of reflection and review, thereby building sustainability and resilience into the team.

However, it is important that we do not see the Five Disciplines as a set of steps to be followed sequentially, but as a map which shows all the disciplines that need to be followed for effective team working. Each team needs to decide, with the help of the coach, which of the issues are most critical to address and in which order, depending on the Inquiry and Discovery conversations, and on what emerges as the work gets started.

8. Peter Hawkins, *Leadership Team Coaching*, pp 52-57

For example:

- If this is a new team then the work would most likely begin by attending to Team Relationships and the process of team building

- If there is a financial or quality crisis then attending to the Team Task round the figures/quality control would be most urgent to attend to

- If the Inquiry revealed that there was a serious breakdown with the primary stakeholder or the employee body then addressing the relationship with the stakeholders might be the starting place.

Of course each of the disciplines affect all the others so while you are working on the Team Tasks, issues to do with Team Relationships will come up as well as impact of the Stakeholder Expectations. The work of the systemic team coach is to support the team in engaging in work that will be serve its growth and performance, working iteratively through the five disciplines as the need arises.

Structuring the Team Coaching Intervention

What does the Execution of Coaching to Fulfil the Development Agenda look like? To optimise the value of the team coaching work we think in terms of four main streams of work, which flow over an agreed period of time, rarely less than six months:

1. Facilitating Workshops that allow the team to stand back and work more strategically or more deeply on how it functions – both task and relationship

2. Business as usual meetings: working alongside the team in its normal business activity, observing, holding the mirror and providing feedback

3. One-to-one coaching sessions

4. Work with the team and their stakeholders in the Connecting and/or Commissioning disciplines.

By working with these four streams, the team coach works collaboratively with the team in an iterative cycle of inquiry, design, intervention, review and learning.

1. Facilitating workshops

This is the favourite mode of engaging with the team around task and relationship issues.

A one or two day event provides the time and focus for the team to really tackle the elements that have been identified on the Development Agenda.

There is a vast amount of material available for facilitating these events both in terms of managing the process and content. We would expect a systemic team coach to be experienced in running these types of workshops or have a co-coach who has the relevant experience. It is beyond the scope of this book to outline all the tools and techniques at your disposal, but the Resources section at the end of this book suggests websites where options are described.

2. Business as Usual Meetings

As we said above that in the Inquiry phase, getting access to observing the team at work provides valuable data. During the Execution phase it is crucial that you arrange to observe the team in its day to day process. This will also enable you to observe the team putting into practice the actions and intentions that they agreed at an earlier off-site workshop.

You need to choose a framework for noting down how the team works. You may already have your own preferred approach, but options include:

- Noting down what everyone says so that the team can review afterwards how the conversations are structured and progressed

- Providing feedback against a behavioural model that the team has developed for itself to guide its process – for example a Red and Green Behaviour Checklist (see the Resources section at the end of this book).

- Observing the types of dialogue that the team uses and how well they listen to each other. You might draw on the work of William Torbert[9], William Isaacs[10] or John Heron[11] to observe types of dialogue.

  For example,

  – How much do team members listen and enquire of each other, as well as advocating a point of view?
  – How well do they build on ideas, respect contributions, as well as offering new thinking?
  – How do they handle conflict and tension?
  – How well do they stand back and look at their own process?

---

9. William Torbert, *Action Inquiry: The Secret of Timely and Transforming Leadership*, Berrett Koehler 2004

10. William Isaacs, *Dialogue and the Art of Thinking Together: A Pioneering approach to communicating in business and in life*, Doubleday 1999

11. John Heron, *Helping the Client,* Sage, 2001

- It is also useful at some point during the observation to sit back and experience the meeting 'out of focus'. What are the patterns in the way that this team discusses, connects and relates? What does it feel like to be part of this team? What do you experience as you listen and observe?

On the Systemic Team Coaching® programmes that we run we practice using a Positive Reflection model where the coach initially comments solely on how effective the team is doing then graduates to commenting on how the team might be more effective if it employed other strategies for relating. There may also be the opportunity to suggest ways of making team meetings more efficient. Again there are numerous resources that can provide guidance or the team just works out its own efficiency plan.

3. One to one coaching sessions

This is an important part of the Systemic Team Coaching® offering and a systemic team coach should also be an experienced individual executive coach. These coaching sessions are intended to help team members stand back from the team work, explore their own development goals in relation to the work of the team, and look at ways in which they can enhance their contribution to the team's shared leadership. These sessions also provide the team coach with information about the priorities for and design of other aspects of the team coaching. It is important to ensure that these coaching sessions are focused on the team work and are not an exploration of their broader personal and professional development needs. It's quite possible that a separate executive coach could be utilised to fulfil this latter function.

4. Working with stakeholders

This is the crucial, systemic part of the Systemic Team Coaching® model and process. As we've said throughout the book, the team is there to serve it's many stakeholders, so ensuring that you have access to them is central to this work.

Ways you might do this include:

- Coaching a team member as she runs her own team session with her direct reports
- Facilitating meetings between the team leader/member and the primary stakeholder or other stakeholder groups
- Helping a leadership team design and run whole staff engagement events and providing feedback for them on their presence and impact at these events.

In most cases the team needs to prepare for their stakeholder engagement and it is valuable that you coach them in how they are going to conduct this meeting e.g., discussion, scenario planning or fast-forward rehearsal. One of the ways that we practice on the Systemic Team Coaching® programmes is to 'step into the shoes of the other' so that the team members get a chance to experience what it's like to being in the other's position.

Tools and Techniques

As suggested earlier, the tools and techniques available for executing the Development Plan are vast. We take for granted that you are an experienced individual team coach because you need the skill required to conduct one-to-one sessions. The ethos of a coaching approach is central to Systemic Team Coaching® work. You need also to have experience in team coaching work already or be working with a co-leader who has the necessary background and experience. We have an on-line resource site that gives you links to many of the tools and techniques we think are relevant to Systemic Team Coaching® practice. See Appendix i in the Resources section at the end of this book.

Phase 5. Review, Evaluation, Learning

Learning through a business-as-usual activity – Core Learning Discipline

One of the gifts that a team coach can bring to a team is the discipline of reflecting on its work and learning from it. Enhanced awareness is the first step to change, and the team coach is instrumental in providing that awareness and holding a safe space in which the team can learn from it.

The slowing down that this requires may be very foreign for a team that is used to rushing from task to task, agenda item to agenda item. You will need to be firm and disciplined in guiding the team in reviewing activity and resolute when there is a tendency to squeeze it from the agenda. This means:

- Providing a process for reviewing learning at the end of every intervention you make – off site, BAU, one-to-one, wider stakeholder intervention

- Helping the team to connect learning from one activity to another

- Sharing your own learning and observations to facilitate the team's own process

- Encouraging individuals to share their personal learning goals in the team as a whole and facilitating supportive and challenging dialogue to help movement towards these goals.

It is important to note that to learn in relationship with others we need to be prepared to be vulnerable with each other – to be less than 'perfect'. In many workplaces that value excellence and achievement it is extremely uncomfortable for individuals or teams to share a sense that they are in any way deficient. The systemic team coach needs to build an environment where the team members feel able to 'let down their guard' and be open to learning and growth.

Formal review and evaluation of the Systemic Team Coaching®

Towards the end of the team coaching programme it is vital to build in time for evaluating the impact of the coaching.

This should take three forms:

- A process by which the team reflects on its own learning and how it will integrate this learning into its work in the future
- An evaluation with stakeholders of the shift in impact of the team, re-running a tool such as the Team Connect 360, or a qualitative process
- A review of any other data that may be indicative of the teams changed impact – employee survey data for example.

It is important to run your evaluation against the objectives set at the outset which indicates the importance of clarifying the objectives at the Inquiry and Development phases. This is similar to the processes you would conduct in a one-to-one coaching context.

Transfer of the systemic team coach role, eyes and ears

A key part of the closing process of the Systemic Team Coaching® work is helping the team to have a simple 'scaffolding' through which it will sustain the practices that have helped it learn and enhance its performance. This might include how they will share responsibility for reviewing their process and team behaviours in Business as Usual meetings and conversations, how they will conduct on-going learning reviews, how they will maintain a constant flow of feedback from stakeholders, and so on.

Summary

This chapter covers the Systemic Team Coaching® Process SIDER Five Phase model:

1. Scoping and agreement with Sponsor and Team Leader
2. Inquiry into the team and its context including methods to use
3. Discovery and Creating a Development Agenda
4. Execution/Coaching to Fulfil the Development Agenda
5. Review, Evaluation and Learning.

CHAPTER

5

DEVELOPING YOURSELF AS A SYSTEMIC TEAM COACH

Questions covered in this chapter

- How do you work as a systemic team coach? Your competence and skills

- Who are you as a systemic team coach? Your Personal Signature Presence

- What underpins and informs your practice? Your distinctive personal approach

- How can we co-lead? What is Parallel Process?

- How important is Team Coaching Supervision?

How do you work as a systemic team coach?
Your competence and skills

Without doubt, Systemic Team Coaching® is a complex process and requires a wide range of skills to be competent.

In Chapter 2 we outlined the six levels of intervention that are open to the systemic team coach (see Fig. 5.1 below)

Fig. 5.1: The six levels of intervention

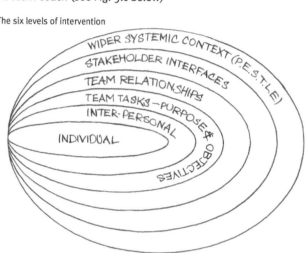

1. Individual
2. Interpersonal Relationships
3. Team Tasks
4. Team Relationships
5. Stakeholder Interface
6. Wider Environmental Impact

Each of these interventions require different skills and the systemic team coach needs to be competent in each one, as well to be able to navigate these levels simultaneously and to judge, in the moment, which level to attend to in order to bring most value to the team.

Underpinning all these is the basic skill of being a coach rather than consultant or trainer. In this book we have taken for granted that a systemic team coach has a fundamental knowledge of and experience in core coaching skills: contracting; building rapport; active listening; questioning; enabling the client to take action: these are the 'lifeblood' of Systemic Team Coaching®

Individual Level

At the Individual level what is required is personal coaching competence. Any executive coaching course accredited by the International Coach Federation, European Mentoring and Coaching Council or the Association for Coaching will provide this. We recommend that a systemic team coach should attain a Practitioner level training (eg. AoEC Practitioner Diploma[1]) and preferably accreditation from one of these professional bodies.

Interpersonal Level

To work at this level needs competence in couples coaching or mediation in addition to individual coaching competence. The work requires creating a safe contained space which enables the two team members to share the personal perspective on their relationship, give each other feedback and explore the factors underpinning tension and conflict in an open and productive way. The coach must demonstrate objectivity and neutrality and be watchful about being pulled to either side of the relationship. Do this by being clear at the contracting stage that your endeavour is to help them improve their relationship in the interest of the business and the wider team, not to help one person shine over the other.

Using personality assessment tools like MBTI or Strength Finder can help a pair to understand different ways of thinking, and provides a vocabulary that makes the sharing of different styles more comfortable and generates greater openness and understanding. It's therefore worth having some training in one of these tools so you can use them confidently and competently.

Managing Team Dynamics

This level requires group facilitation skills that encourages interpersonal dialogue, a building of trust and ability to work with difference and conflict. These skills are more difficult to acquire but by using exercises from the team building repertoire you can create more predictable structures and processes for team exploration. You can hone your ability to identify and work with different types of team dialogue by becoming familiar with one to two models of dialogue. The work of John Heron on Facilitation Styles is helpful here, or the Modes of Dialogue of William Torbert.[2,3]

1. See HYPERLINK "http://www.aoec.com www.aoec.com Practitioner Diploma for accredited coach training courses"

2. John Heron, *The Complete Facilitator's Handbook,* Volume 1, Kogan Page, 1999

3. Bill Torbet and Associates, *Action inquiry,* Berrett-Koehler, 2004

Using team assessment instruments creates another good framework for holding 'courageous conversations'. You'll have seen the Team Connect 360 questions that come from the Co-creating discipline. The data that this tool produces gives rich discussion material that is generally straightforward to manage.

Having experience in Action Learning or Group Coaching will also give you the confidence and competence to work at this level.

One of the best ways of learning these skills is to co-lead with someone who is expert in this area so that you can learn while you practice. Team learning is richest, but also the most complex to manage, when the team is engaged in free-flowing interpersonal discussion. You're 'skiing off-piste', and the challenge and exhilaration of the intervention comes from the spontaneous unpredictable emotional interactions. You need to be comfortable with the expression of feelings to be effective at this level, so that you can stay resourceful at those moments – we'll talk about this later in the chapter.

Team Tasks: Mission, Purpose, Vision, Strategy and Planning

Facilitating the team to address task issues is a more cognitive activity and requires an understanding of business processes and working practices. There are plenty of tools and activities to create a very productive outcome: SWOT analysis for example; so you need to become familiar with these.

Working with a co-leader who has this expertise is the best way to learn, but many of the ideas and practices can be followed from text books. However, to make this effective you do need to be knowledgeable in how to structure the session and be clear about the outcomes. It is also important to be articulate in most of the language used within the client organisation, so understanding the business and its sector are important. You also need to make sure that individuals have taken responsibility for the outcomes at the end of the session so that the learning is transferred back into daily work life.

It would be a mistake, though, to think that this level of team work is just about cognition. The team coach needs to be alert to the emotions that impact on engagement and commitment to such activities. Remember that Clarifying Discipline is about building shared clarity and commitment. That is rarely achieved without the sharing of conflicting views and passions about what the business is about and where it should go.

Team - Stakeholder engagement

Managing the team's relationship with stakeholders requires the same facilitation skills covered above. However it often requires the systemic team coach to have the confidence to push the team to engage with those more senior in the hierarchy in a new and different way. It can be easy to slip into the team attitude of subservience or intimidation in the face of 'powerful' authority figures and allow the team to neglect this. The Team Connect 360 tool creates a starting point for conversations with primary stakeholders (bosses) in the disciplines of both Commissioning and Connecting.

Part of your job as the systemic team coach is to focus awareness on which stakeholders are not being consulted or included in the team's work together. Creating a Stakeholder Map (see chapter 2) with the team can surface awareness of those people in the periphery of the team that may have a big impact. For example, BP in the Bluewater Horizon oil well explosion did not anticipate that local fishermen could bring down the CEO, Tony Hayward.

Wider Systemic Influences

The systemic team coach is not required to know everything about the wider business context of the team: the PESTLE (Political, Economic, Social, Technological, Legal, Environmental) factors. However, your job is to constantly draw the team's attention to these influences to ensure that there is not a blind spot that will catch them out. It's often good practice to keep an eye out for local or international news stories that may affect your team. One very current in the UK at the time of writing is Brexit – the UK withdrawal from the EU. The systemic team coach just needs the courage to ask the obvious and seemingly silly questions about the team's attention to these factors.

Who are you as a systemic team coach?
Your Personal Signature Presence

How you 'show up' as the coach is of critical importance. Being able to build rapport is part of learning to be a skilful individual coach but at team level the complexity is multiplied. You have to build confidence in the individuals as well as in the collective team so that you are able to work with them and their difficulties or tensions.

You need to develop a sound awareness of your strengths and weaknesses so that you're prepared as much as you can be for hitting your limitations. Having a co-leader with complementary skills makes this much easier and models good team work.

Your Signature Presence has five components:

1. Context and contract for the relationship
2. Communication and presentation style
3. Competence to deliver
4. Being centred or being present to do the work
5. Confidence in who you are.

1. The context and contract for the relationship

At a high level, this is about making sure that you have a clear understanding of what you're there to do (or not do) and what the team and organisation expects of you. This is why the first phase of Contracting followed by Inquiry and Discovery is so important. You get a real understanding of what's required and whether you can deliver it. So when you're re-contracting you are confident that you can deliver to expectations.

On a very practical level it's important to ensure that the context for the team meetings fits the work you're intending to do. Do you need them round a table or in a circle of chairs? Are the facilities suitable for the task in hand – basics like refreshments, toilets, lunch? A team that needs to build trust needs a very different environment from one where the team is involved in a business planning activity.

2. Communication and presentation style

Holding the attention of a team or group is challenging, especially if they are uncomfortable with what you're proposing or impatient to 'get on'. It requires you to be able to use your voice, gestures and energy appropriately to help the team to effect the shift of perspective and context they need to make.

On a basic level, you need to understand your group communication preferences, for example, PowerPoint slides or flip charts for delivering input. Have your materials prepared so you get your message across clearly. Be prepared to give clear instructions for exercises. Sometimes these small elements can destabilise a group so that they lose confidence in your leadership and the situation becomes problematic.

3. Competence to deliver

This is about your authority and gravitas and about having a robust theoretical framework as well as the necessary knowledge, skill and experience to deliver what is required on each of the six levels of intervention. Your authority will help the team to put their trust in you: your knowledge and experience and your ability to maintain a safe and contained space for the work.

On the AoEC Certificate Programme of the Systemic Team Coaching® course, you will get a good grounding in the application of the Five Disciplines Model outlined in Chapter 3. On our one year Diploma programme you're required to develop your own Systemic Team Coaching® model of practice (see page 71). You also need to know your limits and capabilities and don't over-promise. As you'll have seen, Systemic Team Coaching® has a very wide and complex range of skill requirements, so be prepared to bring in a colleague to fill the gaps in your own practice. If you have contracted effectively you'll be able to explain your strengths and how you'll fill in the missing elements. While you can always be up for new learning and honing your skills, make sure these are appropriate and discrete elements of your team coaching so you're predominantly in your competence comfort zone.

4. Being centred and being present

At a practical level this means making sure that you are able to fix and maintain your full attention on the team that you are coaching, while keeping in mind the context in which it works. It requires you to pay attention to your internal 'chatter' and any external issues that might distract you and prevent you from being fully present and resourceful. There is a growing body of work on mindfulness available to read. For an introduction to mindfulness, read Jon Kabat-Zin, Mindfulness for Beginners: Regaining the present moment in your life, and Micheal Chaskalson and Mark McMordie, Mindfulness for Coaches.[4,5,6]

You may be a person that works best when relaxed or you may need the buzz of adrenalin to be really present and engaged. You need to work out your own 'mindfulness' routine that gets you into the coach/facilitator 'zone'.

4. Jon Kabat-Zin, *Mindfulness for Beginners: Regaining the present moment in your life*, Boulder Colorado, 2016.

5. Mark Williams and Danny Penman, *Mindfulness A Practical Guide to finding peace in a frantic world*, Piatkus, 2011.

6. Michael Chaskalson and Mark McMordie *Mindfulness for Coaches*, Routledge, 2017.

We believe that this is particularly important because we know that it is in the heat of a tense moment, or in the silent pauses of a meeting, that the team experiences greatest learning – the transformational shift that will move it to a next level of performance. Being effective as a systemic coach requires us to be prepared to slow down the team process, to recognise tension and conflict as data from the system and to stay curious and in connection with everything that is going on. This requires a more profound level of 'presence' than normal, and the ability to tune into the unspoken, unconscious mood of the team. Then through your own physical or somatic experience, to recognise the energy of the team and how you go about using that information to intervene effectively. This will be covered in more depth below, on using your Self as an instrument.

5. Core Confidence in who you are

This is a very personal issue and is all about self-belief. If you have a strong internal critic or 'doubting twin' that undermines your self-confidence then you need to engage in some personal coaching (or maybe therapy) to change that. There are lots of exercises and activities that will help you bolster your confidence but the key is self-awareness – knowing what is likely to trigger a drop in confidence and how to manage it. If you have the other four components in place then this will support your confidence and authority to take the team into the difficult and delicate areas.

As a systemic team coach it is important that you learn that emotional tension or expression in the team is often a manifestation of something in the system. It is important that you do not take this personally as an expression of your own incompetence, but as a data to be worked with in the team. Staying curious at these moments is often the most helpful way of staying present and resourceful with the team.

If you are constantly attentive to these five components then your Signature Presence will grow in strength. This means the team will trust your leadership and follow you into the difficult and unclear areas and therefore produce the richest insight and learning.

By practising in this way you are also acting as an effective role model for the team members and the designated team leader.

Using your Self as an Instrument: Facilitation Map

As we've said above, presence is much more than how professional you are as a team coach. It includes how 'grounded' you are in yourself and your work. It is the ability to be aware of what is going on within yourself and between yourself and the team in the here and now, and to be prepared to articulate some of this to the team so that you can engage in a powerful way. You do this of course in the service of their awareness. Once developed, this becomes a way of life for the team coach, but developing this capacity requires a complex set of capabilities.

The Academy of Executive Coaching Faculty for Systemic Team Coaching®[7] has developed a process that helps the team coach become as 'present' as it is possible to be with a group or team. The steps illustrated in Fig. 5.2, below, make up the seven-step facilitation map:

Fig. 5.2: The seven-step facilitation map

Step 1: How do I broaden my sensory channels/lenses?

From the minute we engage with the team we are already seeing them through our established lenses: our assumptions about what 'healthy team functioning' is and our framework that describes group process, etc. Step 1 invites us to:

• Become more aware of what our lenses, assumptions and biases are

7. John Leary-Joyce, *The Fertile Void: Gestalt Coaching at Work*, AoEC Press, Chapter 9 (By Marion Gillie).

- Put them to one side, so that we might be able to stay with the 'raw data' before moving too early into interpretation
- Learn how to broaden our sensory channels, e.g.: looking out at the team and turning inward to experience our own reactions by fully using our different senses: visual (seeing their non-verbal patterns), auditory (hearing their images and metaphors), sensory (your own somatic reactions and experience of the energy patterns).

Step 2: How do I stand naked in front of the data?

Standing naked in front of the data means adding nothing of one's own 'stuff', i.e. no interpretations, evaluations, hypotheses, no self-talk. This is about learning to distinguish between 'data' and inference/interpretation/intuition. It is the difference between saying "members of the team often speak at the same time" (a description of the phenomenology) and "team members interrupt each other" (an evaluation) or "they are so keen to get their view across they don't listen to each other" (an interpretation).

Step 3: How do I attend to the dance, as well as the dancers?

This requires us to 'see' as opposed to 'look'. 'Looking' implies that we are looking out for something, which is inevitably done through some model (e.g. looking to see what roles the team members adopt). Here we need 'soft eyes' – to wait for the pattern to emerge as a figure from the ground. We are attending to the relationships between people rather than being drawn in to focus on the people themselves. Useful metaphors that help the systemic team coach tune into this way of seeing include, 'if this were a dance, what kind of dance would it be?'; 'if it were music, what would it be?' etc.

Step 4: How do I use myself as a lens?

This is the ability to be in the here and now i.e. to tune into what is going on within yourself (your reactions to the team, what is evoked in you, what images or metaphors come to mind, what sensations are stimulated) as you are affected by them, and to disclose some of this in the service of their learning. Philosophically and theoretically it is based on the notion that these reactions have arisen within the interaction of the current system – of which you are a part – therefore it is reasonable to assume that is has some relevance to them. An important feature of this step is to explore what impact your disclosure has on them and whether it makes sense to them.

Step 5: What is the team-coach dance?

Step 5 requires you to hold in your mind that, as coach in the room with this team, you are also a part of their current system. This can give you another rich source of data if you are able (for a moment) to mentally stand back and consider what kind of pattern or dance is unfolding between you and the team? Do they tend to wait for your guidance or interventions? Do they push back on everything you say? Do some push you whilst others try to rescue you? Do they sometimes act as though you don't exist?

In reality there tends to be an oscillation between steps 4 and 5, i.e. you notice your own reaction evoked by the team dynamics (Step 4) which prompts you to get curious about the team-coach dance (Step 5), then back to Step 4 as you check out your part in the dance. This enables you to speculate on the 'parallel process' and ask: is what's happening in the room mirroring what happens 'out there' between the team and other subsystems in their organisation? As in Step 4, the art then lies in deciding which of these observations to disclose to the team, in the service of their learning.

For Example:

Team Coach: *"As I have been watching and listening to you in the last ten minutes, I have become aware of a strong image as I hear you talk about your current project... I pictured you all engaged in a kind of jive dance, except there were moments of fluidity when you all seemed to know the movements without effort, and then a long period where you were bumping into each other, or missing the hand clasps..." (pause for reaction... then if little or no reaction...) "Does that image have any meaning for you in relation to the project?"*

Step 6: How do I use the lenses to help me and the team make sense of the data?

Step 6 refers to your sense-making through the lenses of the theoretical models and experiences that you bring to your work, the very ones that you were required to put to one side in Steps 1 and 2. By this stage you can use the models more 'cleanly' – your choice of lens is now informed by the data that you have gathered (and can guide your sense-making). Had you used them earlier they would certainly have narrowed the focus of your data gathering.

Step 6 will include sharing those lenses or models with the team, getting their buy-in to them and working with them in collaborative inquiry and sense-making. It will also include broadening your own range of ways in which you engage the team members in this process of sense-making, which brings us to Step 7.

Step 7: How do I intervene to make use of the data?

Up until now we have been exploring different ways of engaging with the data (gathering it and making sense of it). Step 7 is concerned with the many ways in which you can intervene with a team to take their awareness and meaning-making forward.

This might include:

- **Sharing the phenomenological data:** "A pattern that I have been seeing that you may not be aware of is...(describe the data)"

- **Coach Presence and use of self:** disclosing your own reactions and responses as a way of sharing information and raising their awareness;

- **Active experimentation:** offering a process of exploration, via an experiment, to try out, that enables their patterns of interaction and team dynamics to be iluminated, such as Constellations (taken from Bert Hellinger's work on Family Constellations)[8] Sculpting (taken from the world of psychodrama),[9] or methods from Transactional Analysis (e.g. working with the drama triangle, etc).[10]

As well as these existing methods there are also those that you create in the moment with the team, and in these you are limited only by your own imagination and bravery! Such experiments would typically arise from picking up the language and metaphors used by the team and exploring whether they are interested in 'playing' with the metaphor (e.g. 'it feels like we are wading through treacle...' or 'we are forever going around in circles...') might lead to some interesting work with them actually trying this out in the room!.

---

8. Bert Hellinger and Joy Manne, *PhD Family Constellations: A practical guide to uncovering the origins of family conflict,* North Atalntic Books, 2009.

9. Karp, M, Holmes, P, and Bradshaw-Tauvon, K (Eds.), *The Handbook of Psychodrama,* Routledge, 1998. Also see the section on Psychodrama in Hawkins, P, (Ed) *Leadership Team Coaching in Practice,* Kogan Page, 2014.

10. James, M and Jongeward, D, *Born to Win: Transactional Analysis with Gestalt Experiments,* Da Capo Press, 4th Edition, 1996.

What underpins and informs your practice - your distinctive personal model of Systemic Team Coaching®

Each of us who practices Systemic Team Coaching® starts with our own unique set of experiences and perspectives. Some of us come from a one-to-one coaching background, others from organisational development and leadership development; many will have led teams in their careers, and will have experienced different organisational settings. Other aspects of our backgrounds are the theories and approaches that inform our outlook on the world and on how people in organisations relate, behave, change and grow. We believe that the journey of growing our skill, competence and presence as systemic team coaches depends on our ability to be more aware of the experience and learning that we bring to the craft, since they form our lenses on the work of the team and help to constitute our unique approach.

This is why we require all our Diploma students to develop their own signature model and approach when they study with us. Like our students, in order for you to be clear in your knowledge and competence you need to be able to articulate what brings you to the practice of Systemic Team Coaching®

- Your background experience, both personal (e.g.,sports, family) and professional, that relates to team work

- Individual coaching and adult development models

- Knowledge of organisations, leadership, teams

- Understanding of the Five Disciplines Framework and the Systemic Team Coaching® process outlined in this book and also Leadership Team Coaching[11]

- Other theories and models you have learned, some which you have incorporated into your thinking and practice and some you have discarded (these may be relevant at a later stage)

- Your signature approach now, and how is it supported by your practice and unique client experience

- Your learning edge now, and how are you planning to take that learning to the next level.

The task of developing as a systemic team coach is never done – we grow with every experience and every team.

11. Peter Hawkins (Ed), *Leadership Team Coaching in Practice*, Kogan Page, 2014.

Co-leading and Parallel Process

Working with a co-leader has many advantages

- You have another pair of eyes and ears to attend to what is happening

- This gives you another perspective, interpretation, hypothesis on the data collected

- You model good team work by sharing the leadership role and collaborating to make the best use of your diversity as the coaching team

- Being different personalities you are less likely to be emotionally caught by the same 'hook' put out by the team

- It's good to have a colleague to bounce reactions off in a debrief session

- Planning and structuring the engagement with another person adds depth and richness

- It's (usually) more fun and less stressful (see below).

- You can make productive use of the phenomena of Parallel Process (see below).

The downsides of co-leading are:

- It is more expensive for the client with two coaches to be remunerated

- It is time-consuming: you need to set aside more time to plan and debrief

- The need to discuss decisions and interventions will likely surface differences and conflicts that need to be resolved (this can prove to be very productive if worked through effectively)

- You may not get on well enough with your co-leader so the fun element will be missing and this can lead to a different type of stress (as above – supervision can be very productive here)

- Unless you contract very carefully with your co-leader you can get in each other's way in the coaching and fail to deliver your collective value.

From our experience the value of co-leading far outweighs the downsides so we highly recommend it when possible.

Parallel Process in Co-leading

There's a strange phenomenon that occurs in systems that we can utilise to our advantage: that patterns in relationships can replicate themselves in different ways in the system, or in this case, between co-leaders. In some ways this is not a surprise: we know that if the senior team is fractious and dislocated it will spread this attitude through their behaviour and attitude round the organisation.

However there is a much more subtle and unconscious level at which this process operates that systemic team coaches, if aware of it, can utilise very effectively. By paying close attention to the dynamics between the co-coaches, some of the less conscious dynamics of the team members can be identified.

So, if there is an unproductive dynamic happening between the coaching pair, a supervisor can help them sift through this and work out what they need to do on an interpersonal level to be constructive in their difference. Another way of looking at it is to approach their fractious relationship as a reflection or parallel process that is happening within the team but being denied or suppressed by them. Usually if this is parallel process is acknowledged or named in the coaching pair there will be an 'Aha' of recognition and an easing of the tension between them. This then alerts the coaching team to where they need to focus attention: the unspoken dynamic between team members.

How you make the intervention is then up to you but it's extraordinary how often it occurs that at the next meeting the team somehow manages to address the issue reflected in the parallel process.

For example:

The team is outwardly harmonious and agreeable but the team coaches find themselves being irritated with each other and unable to accommodate their differences. In supervision they recognise the over-compliant nature of the team and they wonder where the rebellious, challenging element is. At the next meeting the team coaches plant Lencioni's[12] idea of high performance teams needing to voice difference in ideas (easier generally to start at a cognitive level) and invite the team to explore this issue. This then gives permission for the disaffected team members to voice their views that challenge the prevailing corporate stance.

Individual and Group Supervision

As we've said repeatedly, there is an exciting complexity in Systemic Team Coaching® that often makes it difficult to navigate the most effective way forward. If you are working on your own then this adds further difficulty as you've no other perspective or colleague to bounce ideas off.

12. Lencioni P, *The Five Dysfunctions of a Team: a leadership fable,* Jossey Bass, 2002.

Engaging the support, experience and perspective of a Systemic Team Supervisor is incredibly valuable and in our view essential. While there is extra expense involved, the value added far outweighs this.

A process for exploring the issues and dynamics of a team in group supervision can follow these four steps:

Step One

The coach takes less than one minute to say what success would look like from this supervision

She then talks briefly about the type of team they are working with and some brief data on the team.

Step Two

Group participants take it in turn going round the circle, each asking about the next level of attention; for example:

- **Individuals:** what is happening to the individuals in this team?
- **Interpersonal:** what is happening in the spaces between the individuals?
- **Team Dynamic:** If this team was a piece of music, a meal, a place in the world what would it be?
- **Team Mission and Intent:** What do the team want, need or aspire to achieve that is currently beyond their reach?
- **Stakeholder engagement:** Who are the key stakeholders the team need to engage with and what needs to shift in each of these relationships?
- **Wider systemic context:** What is the shift the team wants, needs or aspires to create in its wider systemic context and what needs to shift in the team so as to bring about the change they want to see?

Step Three

The coach works on clarifying the three-way contract and intent and decides where on the coaching continuum the work with the team needs to focus next:

- The coach becomes the team and states what it (the team) wants from the team coaching and the team coach
- As the systemic team coach, explore what your own intent, interest and investment is in working with this team?

- The coach becomes the organisation in which the team exists, and states what it wants or needs from the team coaching? What is its (the organisation's) view of the return on the investment? How does it want to stay engaged with the process – outcomes?

Step four

The systemic team coach develops the shift required in team and team coach:

- What is the shift needed in the team to meet the aspirations of all parties?
- What is the shift required in my relationship with the team?
- What is the shift required in me (the coach), to bring about the change I want to see?
- What is my specific commitment?

Summary

This chapter recognises that developing as a systemic team coach is a life long journey

- It involves deepening our own awareness of how we engage one-to-one, in teams and with systems, in order more skilfully to help our clients do the same
- Building a discipline into your personal development is fundamental to growing personally in this work. We recommend anyone who is aiming to grow as an systemic team coach to keep a journal of their experiences and their impact
- Most of all, we grow through our contact and relationship with others. So investing in a programme where you can test out your skills with others, and co-lead Systemic Team Coaching® assignments with other skilled coaches, is, we believe, the best way to learn and grow.

6

COACHING TO BUILD COLLECTIVE LEADERSHIP AND SYSTEMIC RELATIONSHIPS

Questions covered in this chapter

- What do we really mean by 'collective leadership' and how might we recognise it?

- How does developing 'collective leadership' differ from developing leaders?

- How can we focus our coaching on developing collective leadership?

- What is the place of the team leader in the Systemic Team Coaching® process?

- How can we build a relationship with the team leader that models shared leadership?

Coaching for Leadership not Leaders: what do we mean by collective leadership?

Example: Hilary

As part of a Systemic Team Coaching® engagement, I was observing the monthly operational management meeting. A day prior to the meeting a document, two centimetres thick, was issued, containing the papers for the meeting. The executive team members sat around a very large oval table, with hole in the middle, the CEO at the top of the oval. As the meeting progressed I observed that the pattern of conversation consisted solely of the CEO 'walking' through the papers, and questioning each respective member of the executive on the sections that related to their area of responsibility. There was negligible dialogue between executive members, but where this did happen, it entailed them advocating opinions, which were directed at the centre of the table rather than to any specific individual. The result was that there was an absence of relational dialogue, and little tangible debating of ideas to create new thinking. Instead, the disparate opinions seemed to fall into the hole in the middle of the table, never, it seemed, to be seen again. Where individual executive members were challenged by the CEO, they seemed to retreat into themselves, tangibly withdrawing from active engagement, as others seemed to wait their turn for CEO scrutiny.

If you have worked with top teams you will most likely recognise this pattern of behaviour, where the CEO holds control and directs through her separate direct reports: The 'hub and spoke' pattern of leadership.

Fig 6.1: The Hub and Spoke pattern of leadership

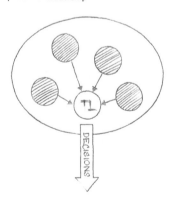

As Barry Oshry points out in his excellent book, 'Seeing Systems'[1], teams at the top of enterprises face a world that is complex and ever changing. In order to deal with this complexity, the top team divides its world into separate functions and assigns individual executive responsibility for those functions (a process Oshry calls 'differentiation'). The key task of the executive team is then to integrate these departments and functions into a strategic whole, bringing individual executive contributions together to create shared leadership which constitutes more than the sum of the parts. If it doesn't, the top team fails to add the value required of its strategic leadership and the differentiation at the top sets a pattern of divisions and silos which fosters unresolved tensions. This pattern is often replicated down the organisation, between departments and functions. Gillian Tett[2] writes very compellingly about the link between such silo mentality and the events that led to the 2007/8 financial crisis.

In order to help a top team develop its shared strategic leadership, the focus of our attention needs to shift:

From	To
The leader as individual	the *connections* between team members in their leadership capacity
Contracting with just the team leader	contracting with the *whole team including the leader* to develop collaborative leadership
The team as an isolated entity	the team *engaging in leadership* in the wider organisation and stakeholder context.

Fig.6.2: Leadership and Systemic Relationships

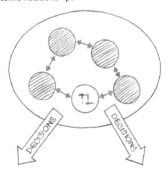

1. Barry Oshry, Seeing Systems: *Unlocking the mysteries of organisational life,* Berrett-Koehler 2007

2. Gillian Tett, *The Silo Effect: The peril of expertise and the promise of breaking down barriers,* Simon and Schuster 2015.c

When working as a systemic team coach in an organisation new to you, it is important that as part of your inquiry, you spend time observing and exploring how the team works. This will enable you to identify the way leadership is owned, shared and conducted both within the team and in its connection with the wider organisation. In addition, collecting data from stakeholders about the team's ways of working will provide you with insight into the cultural context in which the team operates. This will show how the tensions, pressures and behavioural norms of the organisation are re-enacted within the team.

The following examples serve to illustrate other patterns of team functioning that we often see.

Example: The 'Inner Cabinet'

This is an executive team where the CEO establishes a small inner circle of executives who meet more regularly than the whole team and take decisions independently from them. This arrangement can promote team efficiency by minimising the amount of time required of the whole team to make decisions. However, to work well it requires transparency, open communication and trust between the inner cabinet and the outer team regarding the respective roles, decision-making powers and processes of the two sub-groupings. Without this, the inner cabinet can undermine the authority of the wider executive, leading to suspicion, division and disempowerment. The wider organisation soon picks up who has real authority in decision-making and who is marginalised, and this can create disillusionment and disempowerment further down the hierarchy.

Example: The 'Operational Go-Between'

Many enterprises have an Operations Director whose role it is to lead the 'back office' functions. This can become a catchall role into which the CEO delegates all the issues of functional operational concern, so that she can focus on the strategic and stakeholder aspects of her role. This is a potentially efficient way of dividing strategic and operational responsibilities.

However we have seen a situation where the Operations Director took responsibility for both leadership and execution of operational issues, working independently between divisions to get things implemented. One advantage of this approach was that execution of operational actions sat very clearly with one person and his team, and things were dealt with quickly, in the short term.

However, the downside was that:

- *Executive colleagues were ignorant about issues they should have been aware of*
- *These executives were not required to come together to solve key management issues, and so became separated and unaligned*
- *The executive team therefore failed to develop shared strategic and operational leadership, and*
- *Silos were created further down the enterprise.*

In Chapter 5 we discussed the importance of the team leader committing to a change in personal leadership if the Systemic Team Coaching® is to be successful. To fully understand the significance of this, we need to look more deeply at what we mean by 'collective leadership'.

How do we recognise collective leadership?

So what would we expect to see in a team that has shared or collective leadership? Here are some of the things we may notice:

- Energy and alignment around a clear purpose, strategy and goals **(Clarifying)**
- Team members taking responsibility for leading parts of the team's work **(Co-creating)**
- Individual members holding each other accountable for agreed actions **(Co-creating)**
- Consistency between team members in how they represent the team to stakeholders **(Commissioning and Connecting)**
- All members showing active commitment to the growth and development of the team **(Core Learning)**
- A flow of support and challenge between all members, including the team leader, that enables constructive conflict, demonstrates respect and develops trust **(Co-Creating)**.

Shifting our attention from the leaders to the *relationship between leaders*

An example of a lack of shared leadership is illustrated at the beginning of this chapter, where team members showed over-dependency on the team leader and failed to relate to each other in their shared endeavour. Another example was evident when Hilary was observing a leadership team directing an all-staff awayday event. What was striking was not the lack of vision, energy and engagement of the individual executive team members and the Chair that was noticable. Each had their individual style and spoke convincingly with authority and commitment. It was how the space between the Chair and CEO, through body language alone, communicated disrespect, awkwardness and non-alignment. This expressed the distance between them far more loudly than any spoken words. Within hours this fission between them had precipitated a wave of uncertainty throughout the business.The lack of shared leadership was communicated through their relationship.

In their book Touchpoint Leadership[3], Lines and Scholes-Rhodes argue that leadership does not reside purely in the leader or the follower but in the relationship between them. It is the relationship that contains the energy for movement or change to occur – in activities between individuals, groups and organisation systems. In the words of Margaret Wheatley[4]:

"In organisations, real power and energy is generated through relationships... the patterns of relationships and the capacities to form them are more important than tasks, functions, roles and positions". Margaret Wheatley, 1992.

These relationships, in turn, comprise multiple 'touchpoints' of connection between the leader and those whom he aspires to lead. These are points of connection across 'difference': different personalities, functions, loyalties, teams, divisions, and so on. The greater the difference, the greater the scope for learning, growth and added value, as long as the leadership behaviour enables this.

So often the reverse is true – difference in organisations engenders loss of value, such as in the form of passivity and deference or resentment and suspicion, as in the two examples above.

3. Hilary Lines and Jacqui Scholes-Rhodes: *Touchpoint Leadership: Creating Collaborative Energy across Teams and Organisations*, Kogan Page 2013

4. Margaret Wheatley, *Leadership and the New Science: Discovering Order in a Chaotic World*, Berrett-Koehler, 1992.

For a leader constantly to engender value at the 'touchpoint' she needs to:

- Be aware of how she brings her best self into relationship with others (what Lines and Scholes-Rhodes[5] call the personal domain)

- Be tuned into the dance of the touchpoint (the interpersonal domain) and able to flex her style to create the conditions for value to be created, and

- Have continuous oversight of the landscape of connections across her team, her organisation and its stakeholder context and be alert to where leadership is required (the organisational domain).

As systemic team coaches, we therefore need to help leaders attend to the relationship touchpoints – that is the connections between the individuals and how these connections create, or fail to create, value. As coaches we need to shift our attention and concern from the effectiveness of the individual leader (as in the focus of one-to-one coaching or most leadership development programmes) to the leadership relationships between:

- Individual leaders' intentions and how they actually show up with others

- The leader of the team and those whom he leads

- The individual members in the team

- The team as a whole and its stakeholders

- Individuals, groups and sub groups across their enterprise – the touch points in that contribute to the shared leadership culture.

Through coaching these relationships, you can help the team ensure that they add value to their collective endeavour.

This requires us to create and hold the space in which difference can be expressed, respected, and in which new thinking can emerge. This means being able to work with the emergent, to stay grounded in the face of ambiguity and to help the team develop these capacities as well.

---

5. Hilary Lines and Jacqui Scholes-Rhodes: *Touchpoint Leadership: Creating Collaborative Energy across Teams and Organisations,* Kogan Page 2013

Coaching the Systemic Relationships – what are the potential traps?

This section applies both to coaching the relationships in collective leadership as well as coaching other relationships in the system.

We have already said that the prime requirement for being a systemic team coach is to be a high quality executive coach. As coaches, we are energised and committed to the development of human beings. We have a skill set that we know helps individuals to be their best, and we naturally seek out opportunities to use that skill set wherever possible.

However, these qualities can also present us with risks as we try to focus on the relationships between individuals rather than the individuals themselves.

Let's look at some of the potential traps and how to address them:

- Feeling the need to 'deliver' rather than focusing on the relationships and attending to the needs of the team as they evolve
- Taking sides
- Being encouraged to deal with 'difficult' people
- Taking over the leadership of the team
- Over-focus on the interpersonal team dynamics
- Over-focus on the team rather than the inter-team dynamics.

1. Feeling the need to 'deliver' rather than focusing on the relationships

Example,s Hilary:

In a supervision session, a systemic team coach supervisee was recounting how a recent team workshop had gone. "It was all going to plan - then it started to go wrong". She proceeded to describe how a lively argument had erupted between two of the participants, and the whole structure of the day was disrupted. " I wonder", I said, "How you would view this situation if you thought that instead of going wrong, it had actually started to go right?" "Ah", she said, "Well, the lively debate did bring into the open a tension that had been present in the team for some time. But it meant that we weren't able to get to the question that the CEO wanted an answer to."

As systemic team coaches, it is sometimes easy for us, in our commitment to help the team to reach a tangible outcome or output, to miss the interactions in the room that reflect the tensions that need to be addressed. Those moments when tensions are surfaced are 'moments of truth' for the team: they help the team, maybe unwittingly, to 'tell the truth' about the dynamic that is out of awareness. These are touchpoints of potential learning and growth for the team. They require you to take time out from the agreed process and to hold open the space where the tensions can be witnessed, explored and understood with new eyes. In this way you will help the team achieve more than the identified goals, because you will be enabling the team to become aware of and address a blind spot which may be one of the key reasons for under-performance.

To manage a process *time out*, the following approach can be helpful:

Step 1: Signal that you intend to take time-out from the conversation

Step 2: Thank the people who have been involved in the tension for having the courage to bring it to the surface

Step 3: Explain why you think it is important to pause and explore this tension, and how you have experienced it

Step 4: Ask team members to metaphorically stand back from the conversation that has just taken place and to share what they have witnessed and how it has felt. Start with the team members who have not been vocal in the tension. Ask people to speak in turn and for others to listen

Step 5: Start to engage the protagonists in the tension by asking them first, what they have heard, and secondly, what they most need from the rest of the team

Step 6: Take a break at any time to give people space to reflect and get perspective.

2. Taking sides

As coaches we are expected to feel and demonstrate empathy with our coachees, even if we dislike the personality of the person in front of us. We work on ourselves to understand this dislike and how we can use it to serve that person.

When working in a team there is greater opportunity for liking some members more than others, especially if their values and attitudes align with our own. This is a natural human response which we have to pay attention to and work with. Supervision can be most helpful here.

The challenge is how to stay objective and find empathy for the individuals we dislike while holding attention to:

- The relationship that is being explored
- The role of both players
- The potential impact of the wider system on this relationship.

The risk of 'taking sides' can be particularly pressing when working with the team leader in relation to the team coaching programme. Examples include:

- The team leader wanting the team to fall in line with their way of thinking: 'Be on my side, and help me to reform them'
- The team leader saying: 'The Board/Chair doesn't understand me …. help me manage them' or 'help them see my point of view'
- Teams saying that other teams are against us: 'Help us to convince them, bring them on board'.

The most challenging response to such requests is, *'My role is to serve you within the system in which you work. If I side with you, it may feel comfortable, but that will only hide the conflicts between you. I will serve you and your business best if I help you and others to work more effectively in relationship whilst maintaining my own impartiality.'*

Questions to help you maintain this impartial stance and not be drawn in to taking sides include:

- How can I best serve this whole system and thereby help the person in front of me to serve the system better?
- If I stand back from this system with soft eyes, what can I see happening in the overall dynamic that is manifested through the experience being described to me here?
- How do my own feelings and responses to what I am hearing help me to understand what is going on in this system as a whole?
- What data do I have and what do I need to collect in order to form a richer picture of this system?

3. Being encouraged to deal with 'difficult' people

When you first work with a client system, it is not uncommon to be told that things would be much easier or more productive and unified if one 'difficult' person wasn't there or was sorted out. Sometimes you are encouraged to adopt the language that members of the system assign to this person. A supervisee once started talking about the 'psychopath' in the team who was making life hell for everyone else. One team leader told me, 'they are getting too powerful and unless they change no one will want to work with them'.

One mantra that we need to hold close at these times is that:

There are no difficult people in this world; only people with whom we haven't found the right communication channel.

Or, in the words of Canon Andrew White[6], the man known as the 'Vicar of Baghdad' and renowned for building understanding between communities in the Middle East:

"Our enemy is someone whose story we haven't heard yet".

As in 'Taking Sides', the challenge for the systemic team coach is to be impartial, to help the team recognise that leadership and team membership is relational and systemic. Behaviour that is considered unacceptable is most often a symptom of an unresolved issue in the system as a whole.

Some questions to ask include:

- What is that person voicing for the system?
- What part do others play in this behaviour pattern?
- What tensions exist in the commissioning and clarifying disciplines of this team's work that can shine a light here?
- What explicit or implicit protocols exist in this team, and what events or actions tend to divert it from doing productive work?

4. Taking over the leadership of the team

Team coaches often ask:

"Should I expect the team leader to stay in role or be a team member, when I facilitate a workshop?"

Our answer is both. It is important that you work with the team 'intact'. This means that the leader is part of the team but as coach you are also temporarily taking on a leadership role, while running the workshop. This allows the team leader to function more as a team member and create a stronger peer relationship. It also emphasises an aspect of 'shared leadership'. However, it is important that we do not usurp the team leader's role and ensure that in the Core Learning the team leader picks up the responsibility that is conferred by the role.

6. Canon Andrew White: *My Journey so far,* Lion Hudson 2016

This requires a subtle dance. We need to look out for situations where the team leader becomes passive and allows us to take full control of the team management. This is easily done if we are used to working as an advisor or consultant where we bring expert knowledge as well as coaching expertise to our intervention. In this situation it is important to consider whether the team leader is:

- Truly capable of holding that role
- Not committed to developing shared leadership in the team, and just going through the motions.

We find ourselves saying things to the team that should be voiced by the leader. In a recent supervision session a supervisee described some tough feedback that she had given to the team. The team leader had been particularly pleased that she had done this. I said, "I wonder whether you might be giving the feedback to the team that the team leader isn't ?" "Yes", she said, "that's true. The team leader avoids anything really challenging in meetings".

5. Over-focus on the internal team dynamics

This trap gets to the essence of Systemic Team Coaching® and differentiates it from other forms of team coaching. The risk is that of being drawn into the interpersonal dynamics of the team – the clashes of personality and style – and of losing sight of the systemic context. There is equally a risk that we can see harmony within a team as a sign that all is well in the system.

It is a core role of the systemic team coach to hold up the systemic mirror – to ask:

- How do the tensions within the team reflect the demands of its organisational dynamics and that of the organisational business eco-system and the wider PESTLE dynamics; Political, Economic, Social, Technological, Legal and Environmental circumstances?
- What tensions in the external environment are not being brought into the team's process and dialogue? What is not being addressed openly in here? How far is the team being 'wilfully blind' to these issues?[7] Where are the critical relationships external to the team, and how, as a systemic team coach, can I help facilitate more effective dialogue in these?

7. Margaret Heffernan, *Wilful Blindness: Why we ignore the obvious,* Simon and Schuster, 2011

Barry Oshry[8] identifies four roles that individuals and teams automatically get hooked into - Tops, Middles, Bottoms and Customers. The evidence is that human beings naturally gravitate to one of these roles in relation to others within a designated authority and control structure. The attitude engendered by the systemic structure makes it very difficult to not to habitually behave in a particular way. The coach can observe the team dynamics through this lens and make appropriate interventions to change it.

Holding the Six Lenses (see Chapter 1) in mind is key to helping us maintain this systemic perspective.

6. Over-focus on the team rather than inter-team dynamics

As systemic team coaches your client is 'the team' and while you will address stakeholder connections, it is usually only through a stakeholder representative. There is the risk that you are tempted to stay with focusing on the team and away from the team-to-team interface. This is much closer to an Organisational Development intervention, where the organisation is the client, so maybe you need organisational consulting experience to feel comfortable in this area. However getting multiple teams in the room to thrash out their connections and blockages can be enormously powerful.[9]

Contracting with the team leader to create collective leadership

Of course, all the above depends on the formal team leader being prepared to explore a new kind of leadership within her team and to experiment with new ways of relating and leading which enables power to be shared more widely within the team. Not all team leaders, even those who are fully committed to a programme of team coaching for their team, will be ready for this. And even when they feel ready, they may not have yet anticipated the potential discomfort that can arise when learning to be different with their team.

An example of this occurred when coaching a team whose leader wanted to help grow the capacity of the team members so that he could delegate more effectively to them.

---

8. Barry Oshry, *Seeing Systems: Unlocking the mysteries of organisational life*, Berrett-Koehler 2007

9. See Hawkins, *Leadership Team Coaching in Practice*, Kogan Page, 2014, Chapter 11, for a case study where he launched the Systemic Team Coaching® process with this form of engagement.

Example

In team meetings, the coach started noticing that whenever there was a space in team discussions, the team leader would fill it, hence removing the opportunity for team members to step up. He just couldn't stand the discomfort of seeing his team members struggle. When the coach held up the mirror to this dynamic, he saw that his knee-jerk behaviour was getting in the way of his fulfilling aspiration for the team. He started to experiment with staying silent. It felt very awkward at first, both for him and his team members, but gradually the shift in engagement and power sharing started to happen.

This story illustrates the type of contracting that needs to take place between the team coach and the team leader to enable the latter fully to engage in a process that will shift the power relationship in the team – the way that leadership is shared. Your aim should be to develop a trusting partnership in which you can support and challenge the behaviour of the team leader not only off-line, but in full view of the rest of the team.

In that way, the team leader – team coach relationship role models the type of support-challenge partnership that is needed for the team itself to build collective leadership.

Summary

The two connected strands in this chapter have covered coaching around Leadership and Systemic Connections.

We caution against focusing too strongly on the team leader and encourage you to see the team as a composite of leaders. The coaching activity is most likely to be around supporting the team leader to 'step down' and the team members to 'step up' to the leadership role when appropriate.

There is also some guidance on how you manage your time in the leadership role when facilitating one of the coaching events or workshops.

In coaching the systemic relationship, we tracked the team, bearing in mind the *Six Lenses* from Chapter 1.

- Being careful about focusing on an individual 'difficult' team member at the expense of the team dynamics
- Attending to the risk of taking sides within an interpersonal relationship
- Holding the lens of the relationships when working on the task
- Watching out for the PESTLE influence
- Coaching the team to learn as a powerful intervention.

7

YOUR ROUTE TO BECOMING A SYSTEMIC TEAM COACH

Questions covered in this chapter

- What training programmes are available to become a systemic team coach?
- How can you make the most of this development opportunity?
- What does the three-day Systemic Team Coaching® Certificate training consist of?
- What does the 12-month Systemic Team Coaching® Diploma training consist of?
- How to build a Systemic Team Coaching® practice.

Effective training programmes

We – Peter, John and Hilary, along with many colleagues have been on an exciting journey together since 2010, developing training programmes in Systemic Team Coaching® both in the UK and internationally. These include:

- One day introductory courses
- Three-day Certificate programmes
- 12-month Master Practitioner Diploma courses (www.aoec.com).

In that time we have learnt a great deal from both our students and our faculty colleagues about what is helpful and what gets in the way in the complex journey of becoming a systemic team coach. Those who were with us on the early courses have been adventurous and generous fellow pioneers, co-creating and developing the craft and the ways to learn it, and we greatly appreciate all their contributions

This chapter is written for you as a prospective programme participant about how you can get the best from the training and develop the craft of Systemic Team Coaching®.

Getting the most from Systemic Team Coaching® training

The most important step before you start this journey is to develop your clear intention. Why do you want to explore Systemic Team Coaching® and become a systemic team coach?

One way is to reflect on the following questions:

- What are you passionate about doing in your professional life and what is the difference you want to make in the world?
- How does Systemic Team Coaching® connect to this purpose?
- How will this training enable you to make a greater contribution?
- What stakeholders will your team coaching serve?
- What attributes, capacities and capabilities will each of these stakeholders need from you?
- What would you like them to be saying in two years from now, about your work with them?

Four pitfalls that can hold you back

Over the years we've run thousands of training programmes and recognise the attitudes and behaviours that can help or hinder your progress. Often it's easier to see those in other colleagues, but this can be an opportunity to examine these projections by asking yourself: 'How might I also be in the position I see in my colleagues?' In fact this is a key part of the learning to be a systemic team coach – reflecting on your behaviour and attitudes, because you will be asking that of your client teams.

1. Attachment to your current competence

You will be joining this programme with substantial experience in at least one of four professional areas: coach, organisational consultant, trainer/facilitator, team leader, or a mixture of them all. These will be your areas of 'Conscious Competence'[1]. You may be employed internally within an organisation or working independently in a coaching, leadership development or consulting business. Either way, when you get together with a group of colleagues, there is a tendency to need to prove yourself, show you're good enough, have the right skills, establish your standing and authority in the group. This creates a state of caution, not wanting to look stupid or make mistakes – a fear of Conscious Incompetence – which can be a barrier to learning. It is useful to remember the Zen story about the student who came to the master to learn from him, he poured a cup of tea and kept pouring till it overflowed, saying "you are already too full. To learn you must first let yourself be empty".

Here are three practices that can help you get there:

- Open your mind to new thinking, aiming to suspend old habits of thought.
- Open your heart and not be attached to your own feelings and perspectives so that you can step empathically into the shoes of others and look through their eyes.
- Let go of control - having to know what to do and always be 'right'.

---

1. One of the stages in the 'four stages of learning any new skill', originally developed by Noel Burch of Gordon Training International in the 1970's, but often attributed to Maslow.

2. Expecting a straightforward and reliable process that you can roll out with client teams

As you'll have read throughout this book, Systemic Team Coaching® is geared to the VUCA world: Volatile, Uncertain, Complex and Ambiguous. We have provided the Five Disciplines framework as a guide to what you pay attention to, but it's not a formula or linear approach that you work through, discipline by discipline. Teams are complex organisms operating in an ambiguous and fluctuating organisational context and the training to be a systemic team coach must reflect that world. You need to learn to manage confusion and uncertainty, so the training programmes are highly experiential and strike a balance between clear guidance and space for the unknown. Similarly our Systemic Team Coaching® Five Phase process, SIDER (Chapter 4), provides a clear structure that helps you organise and manage the boundaries of your interventions, but you also have to be able to flow with the organisation's fluctuating needs, constantly being open to what comes up in the moment.

3. Having the goal of adding new techniques to your toolkit

Along with the desire to have a simple process comes the wish to have neat tools to utilise as required. There is the belief that the more tools you have, the more competent you will be and beneath that is the hope that 'With lots of tools I will never get caught out, not knowing how to respond.'

Some new tools will be provided but the much stronger emphasis is on drawing on your past experience and supporting you to be curious, creative, inventive and resilient. With additional reading, research and peer discussion you will discover new ways to engage and intervene with your client team.

4. The belief that you need to be competent before you do it

Linked to the points above can be a belief that you need to be competent before you start. Yes, you are expected to be competent in a relevant field but the greater learning comes from the not-knowing, and being prepared to let yourself be Consciously Incompetent. If you hang on to the belief that you must always be the expert, you are in danger of losing some of the most important capacities you need to bring to your Systemic Team Coaching® work: vulnerability, uncertainty, humility and curiosity.

The programme provides multiple opportunities to learn new skills, attitudes and behaviours. We use a well-designed team simulation to provide a safe opportunity for team coaching practice, where – most importantly – you can experiment and learn from multiple mistakes! Great systemic team coaches get it wrong constantly, but are able to learn fast in an open and transparent way that provides learning for all parties. On the Diploma course, when you write up your team coaching case study, you will be assessed not just on what you got right but, more significantly, how well you learnt from what you got wrong.

So what does the training consist of?

In short, putting into practice all the elements that are in this book. We aim to bring alive the theoretical material in the chapters, providing exercises and practice sessions to get you experimenting and learning from experience. The faculty provide a combination of coaching, teaching and supervision.

We review the Five Disciplines and Five Phase Process but expect you to have read this book thoroughly and watched webinars to give you the theoretical grounding, so we can swiftly move into applying it in practice.

The Systemic Team Coaching® Certificate programme (which is also Module 1 of the 12-smonth Diploma programme)

This three day programme provides you with the basic understanding of the what and how of Systemic Team Coaching® and is useful for those starting out exploring being a team coach or those who are team leaders and want to be better at coaching their own teams. We endeavour to create a learning experience that is directly applicable to you as a team coach.

Day One begins by seeking an understanding from you and the group on your experience of high performing teams and what beliefs and assumptions you bring about teams to the programme. This helps to generate a connection between participants and bring their knowledge into the room.

Mirroring the engagement with any team, the connecting of members at the beginning to start to build a trusting environment is crucial. So declaring relationships, expertise, background and motivation for being there is voiced and acknowledged. This includes ourselves as facilitators and our plan for the three days so we emphasise the collective nature of our work together.

This takes us into a deeper exploration of how we will work together. How we develop our learning community and move from the customer/supplier dynamic to working in partnership. This encourages you to be self- aware and capable of disclosing appropriately your internal world – the anxieties, fears and mistakes as well as the passions, joys and delights, thereby modelling the competencies of a team coach.

Paralleling the Five Phase Process SIDER model (Chapter 4) we use with client teams, we then agree our learning contract together. This covers the structure of the day, time-keeping, confidentiality the behaviours that will support learning, such as listening, challenging, supporting, risk-taking, open-ness and trust.

The first key positioning activity is reviewing our perspective on 'What is Team Coaching?' as outlined in this book - our definition, the systemic nature, the position in time, as well as the role of the team coach as an enabler.

We then identify and explain the frameworks and models, tools and techniques that we can draw on. This builds on all the material you've experienced in your career to date. It gives a structure to hold the learning experience. Finally we come back to developing our being, our presence both as team members and as a team coaches, creating self – and other – awareness, as well as sense of self as part of the system (Chapters 5 and 6)

To provide client team practice we use a team simulation: Newcom Ltd., as an interactive case study. Occasionally a whole team attends the programme and is willing to be a live case example. On the 12-month Diploma programme the participants already have a live external client to fulfil this need.

We start the simulation by 'meeting' the key sponsor of the team coaching at Newcom Ltd, engaging in the initial Contracting and conducting the first level of Inquiry. The exercise involves getting you to listen to your internal response/reaction – Tuning In, as valid data about the client (Chapter 4). This is the beginning of the Seven Step Facilitation Map 'Standing naked in front of the data' before engaging with your rational analysis or theoretical models (Chapter 5). Questions like:

- What do you hear?
- Where are you curious about?
- What distracts you?
- What connected patterns do you see?
- What do you feel?
- What is your somatic response?
- What are the assumptions you make about people in the system?

The richness then comes from discussing the wide range of perspectives shared by you as observers and the assumptions that you carry which can inhibit the understanding of the client system.

The next layer of exploration is using the simulation to address the primary components of the Hawkins' five disciplines framework (Chapter 3).

Who is in the team and who are the stakeholders? From there the Commissioning can be addressed – how clear is the mandate from the stakeholders to the team?

How the team takes on board the Commission and works to Clarify its purpose and objectives. Tools and techniques, eg SWOT and Team Time Line, will be shared to help surface and resolve the differences that necessarily emerge in order to build the Shared endeavour.

On **Day Two** we move into the Co-creating discipline and this is where you can really experience the elements of this discipline live in the group. While it is a one-off group and not a team, we can explore and experience many of the dynamics of a team as they are happening live in this learning community.

Elements like:

- **Stages of team development** – drawing on models by Tuckman, Schein, Shultz
- **State of a team in time** – new, mature or transitional
- **Location** – face to face, semi virtual, totally virtual
- **Roles and functions** – single and collective leadership, Belbin and MBTI profiling
- **Team process** – Gestalt[2] and the Solution focused approach
- **Methods for working with the team** – Positive Reflection, Five Dysfunctions of a Team (Lencioni[3]), Dead Dog/Secrets Exercise
- **Tools and techniques for team building** – sculpting, constellations, art and storytelling.

The faculty work with the group as a learning community using both structured and unstructured approaches, drawing on the elements above, as appropriate, and using themselves in an intuitive as well a as planned way.

---

2. John Leary-Joyce, *The Fertile Void: Gestalt Coaching at Work*, 2004, AoEC Press.

3. Patrick Lencioni, *The Five Dysfunctions of a Team*, 2002, John Wiley & Jossey-Bass.

Then there is an opportunity for you to put it all into practice and try out these tools and techniques with the Newcom Ltd. simulation team. You can take on a Newcom team character or choose to be part of a pair of team coaches deciding what intervention to practice. Alternatively, you can be an observer along with the faculty members, tracking the process and interventions to provide constructive feedback. Masses of learning happens on all fronts, mostly from failing to deliver a 'great performance' as the team coaches!

Day Three starts by addressing the fourth discipline: Connecting – going back to the Newcom Ltd. simulation to explore and discuss the nature of the relationship between the team and the stakeholders. Re-engaging the Newcom Ltd. team in this discipline provides the opportunity for you to change roles. We draw on the stakeholder map intervention (Chapter 3) to then explore the technique of 'stepping into the shoes of the stakeholder' (Chapter 3). This really brings into strong relief the centrality of the Systemic Team Coaching® – that of really engaging stakeholders.

In the afternoon of Day Three we explore the fifth discipline: Core Learning (Chapter 3). We discuss how we experience this discipline in teams we've been part of and client teams we've worked with. On an immediate level, we focus on looking at our Core Learning over the last three days, both individually and as a learning community. This is charted against the contract and expectations for the programme agreed at the beginning.

To pull the whole theoretical and experiential learning together we split into subgroups of three or four, with one participant presenting a live client example. Using a highly structured sequence of questions, the presenter then is guided through the Five Disciplines model with the others acting as coaches to help apply it to the client example.

This brings enormous clarity as the model comes alive as a real-life team situation. The presenter gains a real shift in thinking and attitude to their team and the support coaches gain a great deal from tracking the process and seeing how and what their colleague is learning about their team.

Finally there is a review of the programme and revisiting the day-one exercise where participants stated what they wanted to learn for themselves and their stakeholders. This clarifies whether your expectations have been met and, if not, what you want to do more of.

The combination of theoretical, experiential and practitioner learning is a powerful and intense combination and participants come away understanding and experiencing the challenge of the task of Systemic Team Coaching®. You will also have acquired a very sound route map to take forward into your team experiences.

The Certificate also licences you to use the Team Connect 360 survey tool that you will have practised using with the Newcom Ltd. simulation team.

One Year Master Practitioner Systemic Team Coaching® Diploma

Having had an overview the Systemic Team Coaching® approach from the Certificate, the 12-month Diploma seeks to embed this through deeper learning and supervised practice. The goal is not to simply learn the theoretical framework and methodology, but to take that perspective and create your own signature model and process within the broad Systemic Team Coaching® framework.

Having developed the essential knowledge about our approach from the Certificate, you will be sufficiently confident to recruit a live team (either paid or pro bono) as your client over the 12-month training programme. The faculty members will offer support and guidance in this process. You have the opportunity to use the Team Connect 360 tool with your client, free of charge both at the beginning Inquiry phase but also again at the end at the Review stage.

There are then three subsequent three-day modules that revisit the SIDER Process and Five Disciplines model in greater depth. There are a number of different configurations constructed for each module that support this learning.

- The whole group (around 20) as a learning community becomes a vehicle for intensive experience of a) a complex system at work, and b) the elements of the Co-creating discipline – facilitated by the faculty acting as team coaches. Much personal insight is gained as we explore how you 'show up' as a community member and how that reflects your stance as a team coach. This learning community also often becomes a forum in which research and literature is shared and discussed between modules.

- The Practitioner Teams (around five to six members) are the context in which you bring your client team for peer and faculty supervision. This gives you enormous support in taking on your first practice team, tracking you through the process and interventions you make with it. These teams become hubs of learning, challenge and support, both on programme modules and between them.

- Practice Sessions are an opportunity to present your client team and have other participants role-play the characters and situation you are facing. Generally one or two of your peers will take on being the team coach while you observe the way the team members act out the situation and how the team coaches intervene.
- Individual Supervision with faculty members gives you intensive coaching on how to be more effective with your team.
- Individual Tutorials between modules help you navigate your personal development through the programme.
- Of course there is faculty input of theory, models, examples and experiential exercises to provide additional perspectives on your thinking and practice. The faculty aim to make these input sessions as dynamic and interactive as possible.

Module 5 is the culmination of this process – we call it Harvesting the Learning. In these two days, you present your signature model and the journey you've been through with your client team to your peers and get their feedback. It also means you get to listen and feed back to some of your other peers – a process which is immensely rich. Again the objective is not to demonstrate your perfect model and practice but to show the learning from the mistakes, blind alleys and frustrations that you've struggled through.

The ultimate goal, as we said at the beginning of this section, is to produce your own signature model for team coaching in a systemic way. This is realised after Module 5 in the final assessment where you submit two papers. First, your signature model – a personal description of the theories, tools and techniques that have appealed to you and illustrate your way of delivering systemic team coaching. Second, your case study – a description of the journey with your team client that shows how your signature model has been applied in practice. We also ask you to submit a short marketing statement, setting out how you will present your Systemic Team Coaching® expertise and services to your clients. We want to support you in growing your business from this investment.

The evolution of this Diploma programme has been an exciting and rich journey for us as faculty and we have greatly appreciated the pioneer participants who helped us to build these refined and well-structured programmes.

For further information on these programmes please see the team coaching pages on our website **www.aoec.com** or drop us a line at **info@aoec.com**

How to build your Systemic Team Coaching® practice

To build a Systemic Team Coaching® practice you need to have:

- **Capability** – which would come from completing the Systemic Team Coaching® Diploma. If you have extensive team coaching, organisational development and leadership experience then integrating the experience and framework from the Systemic Team Coaching® Certificate may give you enough capability. On completing the Diploma, you will have created your own signature model and framework so you will be able to talk confidently about what you can deliver and the process for getting results.

- **Credibility** – this is more difficult as you're just starting your practice. However you will have been a successful and credible individual coach, consultant, developer and possibility team leader and you can utilise this background to show you are reliable and capable of delivering what you claim. The marketing statement you are required to complete for the Diploma will help you demonstrate your credibility especially if backed up with testimonials from the client team work case study.

- **Experience** – as above, when launching your practice, you will have to rely on the experience of the Diploma programme client work and weave that into your credibility from previous professional experience. It will also be good experience and part of your Corporate Social Responsibility commitment to run a pro bono Systemic Team Coaching® programme for a charity.

- **Contacts** – using your network into a preferred client market. This is really about extending your existing client contacts and letting them know you've added Systemic Team Coaching® to your current portfolio. How to market your practice and develop your contact network is a skill that is covered in many books on this subject.

Routes to market for Systemic Team Coaching®

From our personal experience and drawing on the experience of our graduates, we've identified a number of channels you can use to open out the opportunity for Systemic Team Coaching®

- If you are engaged in coaching a team leader, explain the Five Disciplines framework and explore the challenges he faces as a team leader in each of the disciplines. Then introduce the idea of coaching his team. It may be appropriate to offer a copy of this book by way of deeper explanation.

- If invited to do a team building (Co-Creating Discipline) or strategic planning (Clarifying Discipline) workshop, introduce the idea of the other Disciplines and explore how this workshop could be more effective if linked with a wider systemic intervention

- If you've been asked to coach a difficult team member, do some further Inquiry into the systemic context and if your findings confirm it, propose that the solution will be found in teamwork rather than individual coaching.

- If you are part of or involved with an organisational restructuring, propose that Systemic Team Coaching® would be an effective integrating process or a way to speed up the formation and effectiveness of new teams.

- If you are approaching a new client – a team leader or potential sponsor, suggest doing the Team Connect 360 diagnostic survey as a way of identifying the problems and strengths of the team. You can offer this at a very reasonable rate with the expectation that having identified the development areas, the client will wish to hire you to take the work further.

- If your work is part of a culture change programme, suggest that Systemic Team Coaching® would be a powerful way of influencing team culture and that the connection with stakeholders would impact the wider culture.

Of course all these routes to market yourself require you to develop confidence and authority in 'selling' Systemic Team Coaching®. This book will help you think through where you need to focus to build your business, but it will not give you the practice and experience that comes from doing a training programme and working with teams. We'd also like to reiterate that supervision is an essential tool to support you in the initial engagement with potential clients.

We wish you all the very best in your adventures into the field of Systemic Team Coaching.®

Summary

- Outline of the training programmes that are available to become a systemic team coach

- The four pitfalls that will hold you back from making the most of this development opportunity

- Overview of the three-day Systemic Team Coaching® Certificate training

- Overview of the 12-month Systemic Team Coaching® Diploma training

- Four requirements for Developing your Systemic Team Coaching® practice and some suggested routes to market.

Index

Action learning, 62

Active experimentation, 70

Attending to the dance as well as the dancers, 68

Being present, 65, 66

Belbin, 30

Business as usual meetings, (Execution phase), 55, 57

Chartered Institute of Personnel and Development (CIPD), 4

Chemistry, 38

CIDCLEAR, 6 phases, 36

Clarifying team tasks (Discipline 2 of Five disciplines Framework) 7 tasks:

  1. Purpose or Shared Endeavour,25, The Role of the Systemic Team Coach, 26

  2. Vision, 26, The Role of the Systemic Team Coach, 27

  3. Strategy, 27, The Role of the Systemic Team Coach, 27

  4. Objectives and Targets, 27, The Role of the Systemic Team Coach, 27

  5. Systems, Processes and Protocols, 27, The Role of the Systemic Team Coach, 28

  6. Roles and Responsibilities, 28, The Role of the Systemic Team Coach, 28

  7. Values, 28, The Role of the Systemic Team Coach, 29

Co-coaching, working with co-leader, 49, 57, 62, 63, 65, (advantages of) 72

Collaborative discovery, 49

Collective Leadership, 78, 81

Conducting Interviews, 45, 46, 48

Confidentiality, 41

Constellations (Hellinger), 70

Contracting for the work, 49, 51, 52

Contracting with the team, development phase, 50

Developing Team Coaching Agenda, 49

Development agenda (for the team) 51, 53, 54

Difference between a group and a team, 2

Difficult people, 86, 87

Directed Inquiry, 45

Educating and selling Systemic Team Coaching® to a Team Leader, 16, 17, 18

Educating and selling Systemic Team Coaching® to the Team, 17 -18

Emotional tension as data, 66

Facilitating workshops, 54, 55

Facilitation map (seven step) 67

Facilitation styles, 61

Fast-forward rehearsal, 57

Feedback for Team leader, 48

Firo-B tool, 30

Five Disciplines Framework, Chapter 3, p20 onwards, 38, 93

   – Commissioning – Stakeholder Expectations, Discipline 1, 23,

   – Clarifying – Team Tasks, Discipline 2, 25, 7 tasks

   – Co-creating – Team Relationships, Discipline 3, 22, 29

   – Connecting – Stakeholder Relationships, Discipline 4, 31

   – Core learning, Discipline 5, 32 The Role of the Systemic Team Coach, 32

Four-box Team Model, Inside/Outside the Team, (diagram) 20, 21,22

Gestalt (coaching, perspectives) 70

Group Coaching, 3, 62

Group supervision, 73, 74, 75

High performing team, 2,17

Holding boundaries, 45

Hub and Spoke pattern of leadership, 78, 89, 90

Individual Coaching/core to Systemic Team Coaching® differences, 3

'Inner Cabinet' style of leadership and team functioning, 80

Insights tool, 30

Inter-team Coaching, 4

Metaphor (working with), 70

Mindfulness, 65

MTBI (Myers Briggs Type Indicator) tool, 30, 61

Observing the team at work (Inquiry), 49

'Operational Go-between' style of leadership and team functioning, 80

Organisational Development , 4

Other organisational data (Inquiry), 49

Parallel process in co-leading, 72, 73

Parallel Process, 30, 69, 72, 73

Personal Model of Systemic Team Coaching® (signature model and approach), 71

PESTLE, 31, 49, 63, 88

Phenomenological data, 70

Process time out, 85

Psychometrics and Team Assessment tools , 48

Red and Green behaviour checklist, 55

Relationship between leaders, 82, 83, 84

Relationship Touchpoints (leadership), 83, 85

Reviewing and evaluating learning as a systemic team coach, 58

Reviewing team learning, 58

Scenario planning, 57

Sculpting (psychodrama), 70

Self as instrument (using), 67

Self-awareness, 66, 67 onwards

Self-disclosure as a coach, 69, 70

Shared strategic leadership and team functioning, 79

SIDER phases:

    Phase 1: Scoping, Relationship Building and Agreement with the sponsor, 37, Team Leader as Sponsor, 37, Team's Boss as Sponsor, 37, Third Party as Sponsor, 38

    Phase 2: Inquiry into the Team and its context, 42,

    Phase 3: Developing the team coaching agenda and contracting for the work, 49

    Phase 4: Executing and engaging to fulfil the development agenda, 53

    Phase 5: Review, evaluation, learning, 57

SIDER, Systemic Team Coaching® 5-phase Process (Scoping, inquiry, developing team coaching agenda, Execution and engagement, Review), 36, 37

Signature model, 100, 101

Signature presence/personal signature presence, Chapter 5, 63 onwards

Silos, 79, 81

Six Lenses of Systemic Team Coaching®,5-8, 9, 60, 89,90

Skills and competence of a systemic team coach, Chapter 5, 60, 63

Stakeholder engagement (for the team), 57

Stakeholder Map, 21,42,43,63

Stakeholders inside and outside the team, 20, 21

Stand naked in front of the data, 68

Strength Finder tool, 61

'Step into the shoes of the other', 57, 67, 68

Structuring the team coaching intervention, 54, 55

Supervision, 73, 85, 87, 88, 100

SWOT analysis (using), 62, 97

Systemic team coach supervision, Chapter 5, 60 onwards

Systemic (use of term), 5

Systemic perspective in team functioning (see four box model), 20
Systemic Team Coaching® definition, 3, 4

Taking over leadership of the team (as the coach), 87
Taking sides (as a systemic team coach), 85, 86
Team Building, 4, 30
Team Connect 360 tool, 20,23,24,29,31,32,33,46,47,51,62,98,99
Team facilitation, 4, 30
Team Time Line tool, 97
Team-coach dance, 69, 88
Transactional Analysis (TA), 70
Tuning into the client system, 39, 97

Undirected awareness, 40, 67 onwards
Undirected Inquiry, 44
Undirected observations, 49

VUCA (Volatile, Uncertain, Complex and Ambiguous) viii, 94

Who is your client? 16, 41, 89
Working with stakeholders, 56

Appendix i

On-Line Resources

Log in to **www.aoec.com/STCresources** to find a list of links to tools and techniques that we, our colleagues and course participants have used when engaged in team development. We are constantly hearing of new or different tools and techniques so please return for updates and submit any of your own that you have found useful.

Log in to Dr Krister Lowe **www.teamcoachingzone.com** for a wide range of podcasts on team coaching.

Further Reading

Argyris, C (1990) *Overcoming Organizational Defenses: Facilitating Organizational Learning*, Needham Heights, MA, Allyn and Bacon (One of the most readable from Argyris, covering skilled incompetence etc. Unfortunately it's £45 second hand on Amazon).

Block, P. (2002) *The Right Use of Power: How Stewardship Replaces Leadership*, Audio CD/download from Amazon. The Inner Art of Business Series.

Block, P. (2011) *Flawless Consulting: A guide to getting your expertise used*, Jossey Bass, 3rd Edition, April 2011. Classic text in process consulting. Compare this practice with team coaching.

Burke, W. (2002) *Organization Change: Theory and Practice*, London, Sage Publications.

Caulat, G. (2006) *Virtual leadership*. In The Ashridge Journal 360, Autumn 2006.

Caulat, G. and de Haan, E. (2006) *Virtual Peer Consultation: How Virtual Leaders Learn*. In Organisations and People, November 2006, Vol 13, No4.

Clutterbuck, D. (2007) *Coaching the Team at Work*, London, Nicholas Brealey.

Clutterbuck, D. Hayes, S. Lowe, K. Lordanou, I. McKie,D., Editors, (2018) *The Handbook of Team Coaching*, Gower.

Davison, S.C. & Ward, K. (1999) *Leading International Teams*, London, McGraw-Hill.

De Haan, E. (2017) *Team Coaching Pocketbook*, Management Pocketbooks.

Dunne, P. (1997) *Running Board Meetings*, London, Kogan Page.

Gall, J (1979) *Systemantics. How systems work and especially how they fail,* Fontana. (A fun read with cartoons and stories).

Garratt, B. (2010) *The Fish Rots from the Head: The Crisis in our Boardrooms,* Third Edition, London, Profile Books.

Hackman, J. R., and Wageman, R. (2005) *A Theory of Team Coaching.* In Academy of Management Review, 30(2), 269-287.

Hawkins, P. (2012) *Coaching Strategy in Organizations: Developing a Coaching Culture for Improving Business Effectiveness,* Maidenhead UK, McGRaw Hill/Open University Press.

Hawkins, P. (2017) *Leadership Team Coaching: Developing Collective Transformational Leadership,* London, Kogan Page.

Hawkins, P. and Smith N. (2006) *Coaching, Mentoring and Organisational Consultancy: Supervision and Development,* Maidenhead, Open University Press/McGraw Hill.

Hawkins,P (Ed) (2014) *Leadership Team Coaching in Practice,* Kogan Page.

Heifetz, R. (2009) *The Practice of Adaptive Leadership: Tools and Tactics for Changing your Organisation and the World,* Harvard Business Press.

Holbeche, L. (2005) *The High Performance Organisation,* Oxford, Elsevier Butterworth-Heinemann.

Kaplan, R. S. and Norton, D. P. (Jan-Feb 1992) *The Balanced Scorecard: measures that drive performance,* Harvard Business Review.

Karp, M., Holmes, P. and Tauvon, K. B. (1998) *The Handbook of Psychodrama,* Routledge.

Katzenbach, J. and Smith, D. (1993) *The Wisdom of Teams. Creating the high-performance organisation,* McGraw Hill.

Leary-Joyce, J. (2014) *The Fertile Void, Gestalt Coaching at Work,* AoEC Press.

Lencioni, P. (2002) *The Five Dysfunctions of a Team. A Leadership Fable,* San Francisco, Jossey-Bass

Lencioni, P. (2005) *Overcoming the Five Dysfunctions of a Team. A Field Guide,* San Francisco, Jossey-Bass

Lencioni, P. (2006) *Silos, Politics and Turf Wars, A Leadership Fable,* San Francisco, Jossey-Bass

Lines, H. and Scholes-Rhodes, J (2013) *Touchpoint Leadership: Creating collaborative energy in teams and organisations*, Kogan Page.

Lipnack, J. and Stamps, J. (1996) *Virtual Teams: People Working Across Boundaries with Technology*, NY, John Wiley & Sons.

McChrystal, S. and Silverman, G. (2015) *Team of Teams: New rules for engagement in a complex world*, Penguin.

Nevis, E (1997) *Organizational Consulting: A Gestalt Approach*, Gestalt Institute of Cleveland Press.

Oshry, B. (1999) *Leading Systems: Lessons from the Power Lab*, San Francisco, Berrett-Koehler.

Oshry, B. (2007). *Seeing Systems: unlocking the mysteries of organizational life, 2nd Edition*, San Francisco, Berrett-Koehler.

Price, C. and Toye S. (2017) *Accelerating Performance: How organizations can mobilise, execute and transform with agility*, John Wiley & Sons.

Scharma, C. O. (2007) *Theory U: Leading from the Future as it Emerges. The Social Technology of Presencing, Cambridge*, Society for Organisational Learning.

Schein, E. H. (2003) *On Dialogue, Culture, and Organisational Learning.* In Reflections, 4(4), 27-38.

Senge, P. Jaworski, J. Scharmer, C. and Flowers, B. (2005) *Presence: Exploring Profound Change in People, Organizations and Society*, Nicholas Brealey.

Senge, P. Kleiner, A. Ross, R. Roberts, C. and Smith, B. (1994) *The Fifth Discipline Fieldbook: Strategies and Tools for Building a Learning Organization*, Nicholas Brealey Publishing.

Thornton, C. (2010) *Group and Team Coaching*, Hove, East Sussex, Routledge.

Ulsamer, B. and Beaumont, C. (2003) *Art and Practice of Family Constellations: Leading Family Constellations as developed by Bert Hellinger*, Carl-Auer-Systeme-Verlag (it is in English).

Wageman, R. Nunes, D. A. Burruss, J. A. and Hackman, J. R. (2008) *Senior Leadership Teams*, Harvard Business School Press.

Recommended Reading specifically on Co-Creating Discipline and Team Relationships

Adair, J. (1986) *Effective teambuilding. How to make a winning team,* Gower Publishing Ltd. (a useful historical perspective).

Belbin, M. (2004) *Management Teams: Why they Succeed or Fail,* London, Heinemann.

Bion, W. R. (1961) *Experiences in Groups, London,* Tavistock.

Bird, J and Gornall,S. (2016) *The Art of Coaching: A Handbook of Tips and Tools,* Routledge.

Dyer, W.G. Dyer, W. Gibb, Jr. & Dyer, Jeffery, H. (2007) *Team Building. Proven Strategies for improving team performance,* Jossey-Bass

Gratton, L. and Erickson, T.J. (2008) *Eight Ways to Build Collaborative Teams.* In Harvard Business Review (online version: https://hbr.org/2007/11/eight-ways-to-build-collaborative-teams/ar/pr, 05/02/2008).

Hunter, D. Bailey, A. and Taylor, B. (1996). *The Foundation of Groups,* Hampshire, Gower.

Katzenbach, J., and Smith, D. (2001) *The Discipline of Teams: A Mindbook-Workbook for Delivering Small Group Performance,* John Wiley & Sons.

Kegan, R. and Lahey L. (2009) *Immunity to Change: How to overcome it and unlock the potential in yourself and your organisation,* Boston, Harvard Business School Press (sets out protocols for working both with individuals and whole teams, very practical and wise about getting started with teams).

Kegan, R. and Lahey, L. (2016) *An Everyone Culture: Becoming a deliberately developmental organization.* In Harvard Business Review

Kets de Vries, M. F. R. (2005) *Leadership group coaching in action: The Zen of creating high performance teams.* In Academy of Management Executive, 19(1), 61-76.

Levi, D. J. (2010) *Group Dynamics for Teams, Sage,* 3rd Edition.

Palmer, W. and Crawford, J. (2013) *Leadership Embodiment: How the way we sit and stand can change the way we think ad speak,* Createspace.

Schein, E. H. (1969) *Process consultation: Its role in organisational development,* London, Wesley.

Smith, K. K. and Berg, D. N. (1997) *Paradoxes of Group Life: Understanding*

Conflict, Paralysis and Movement in Group Dynamics, Jossey-Bass Business and Management.

Tuckman, B. (1965) *Developmental sequence in small groups.* In Psychological Bulletin, 63(6), 384-399 (for historical interest).

Western, S (2013) *Leadership: A Critical Text,* Sage.

Whitelaw, G (2008) *Move to Greatness: Focusing the four essential energies of a whole and balanced leader,* Nicholas Brealey.

Team Connect 360

Team Connect 360 is a powerful diagnostic tool which will give your team new and valuable insights into how they can be more effective and productive in your organisation.

It is special in having questions that address external connections with six stakeholder groups, as well as internal connections between team members, and how they relate to their team purpose, strategy & targets.

The Questionnaire and Report focus on six areas:

- **Stakeholder Expectations** What the team is required to deliver

- **Team Tasks** What the team does to meet those expectations

- **Team Relationships** The interpersonal and leadership dynamics

- **Stakeholder Relationships** How the team connects with those it serves

- **Team Learning** How the team develops to meet future challenges

- **Overall Productivity** Summary of the team's record on capacity to deliver.

This gives a clear picture of how well the team is connected within its organisational system and what it can do to be more effective.

The Team Connect 360 Report is an excellent tool to focus external consultants or team coaches on where they can add the most value.

5 Disciplines for Team Effectiveness

1. Meeting Stakeholder Expectations

For your team to be successful you need a clear directive on what is required from the stakeholders you serve. This includes a clear purpose and defined success criteria by which your performance as a team will be assessed. It will be for your primary stakeholder (individual/team/group that the team reports into) to define your primary commission and for you to negotiate the final terms. In addition, your other stakeholders (peers, reporting teams, clients, customers and suppliers) will have an influence on how you as a team are expected to perform and the way your success will be measured.

2. Fulfilling Team Tasks Effectively

Having ascertained what your stakeholders require, you need to jointly clarify how you will execute it. To be effective, you have to create a collective endeavour that is both challenging/compelling/rewarding and can only be achieved by all of you working together. In this section the responses show how well you have created this joint endeavour and how aligned you all are in your stated purpose, goals and values. The data will also show to what extent the roles, responsibilities, accountabilities and processes serve the achievement of goals, and the fulfilment of the team's role in the organisation.

3. Building Collaborative Team Relationships

This discipline focuses on how to achieve more as a collective unit rather than as separate individuals. This requires you to maximise the different skills, experiences, specialisms and styles within your team so you can generate new thinking and actions for the benefit of your stakeholders. The data will indicate how well you work together as a team to achieve the shared endeavour, including the nature of leadership, and where your behaviours and patterns get in the way of joint effectiveness.

4. Connecting Well With Stakeholders

Your team will only make a difference to the organisation when you collectively connect and engage with all your stakeholders. These stakeholders need to be managed effectively in order to achieve your purpose, objectives and commission. The data in this section will demonstrate how well you as a team relate to, and provide leadership for, these individuals and groups.

5. Becoming a Learning Team

If you as a team are to make the best of your skills and resources you need to take time to reflect on your individual and joint performance. You need to review what you are collectively learning from your successes and failures and how you can use this learning to enhance your performance in the future. In this section respondents are telling you how well you as a team are capturing the learning for the benefit of organisation, as well as how it nurtures and encourages the learning and development of each team member.

The 360° Questionnaire

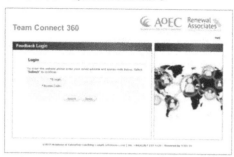

Online questionnaire, login page

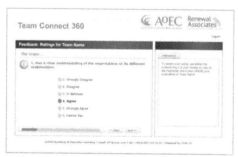

Online questionnaire, question page

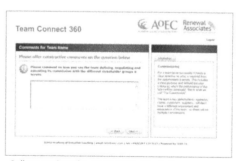

Online questionnaire, open ended comments page

Process Steps

1. Initial communication to the team and its stakeholders to position the exercise

2. Team coordinator provides details of those participating in the feedback exercise;
   - Primary stakeholder
   - Team members
   - Reports to the team
   - Three other stakeholder groups

3. Invitation emails with web links are sent out for on-line completion

4. A short, focused questionnaire about the team and its interactions and outcomes is completed

5. Feedback is aggregated into a report

6. Meeting with Team Coach and Team Leader to discuss the results

7. Meeting with the whole team to share and debrief

8. Plan actions for change based on results

Outputs

The feedback results are reported back in a direct and visual manner for speed and ease of interpretation, to focus on the key priorities and drive action planning for improvement.

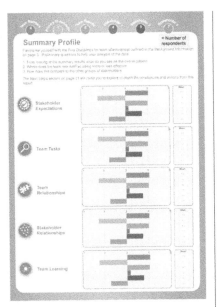

Detailed Analysis for Each Discipline

The responses to each question are collated into colour coded graphs (not B&W as illustrated here). Note that the last two questions in each section are directed to the team members, so only answered by them.

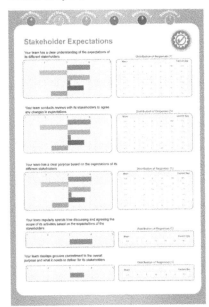

Summary Profile

An overview of the Five Disciplines indicating what is and isn't working well for the team, reporting the perceptions of the different respondent groups.

Written Commentary From Respondents

Respondents can also provide written feedback under each Discipline. This is also collated and colour coded so it's clear from which group the feedback belongs

For further information, and details of fees and coaches licenced to administer the Team Connect 360, contact:

Mike.Smith@aoec.com   Tel 0208 916 9063

Appendix iii

Example Inquiry Questions for the Team

Team's commission:

- What are the key external challenges that the business faces currently and in the next two years?
- What are your key stakeholders demanding of you?
- How would you describe the task that the primary stakeholder requires you to fulfil?
- What are the strengths of the team's relationship with the primary stakeholder and what needs to shift to create enhanced clarity of purpose, partnership and shared leadership?

Strategy, purpose, role:

- What is your personal hope and vision for the business in the next 2-3 years?
- How far does the team have a clear strategy to fulfil this vision?
- How far are the purpose, vision and strategy jointly owned by the whole team?
- What do you need to achieve by when and how will you measure and demonstrate tangible progress?
- What needs to shift for you to execute your strategy more effectively?

Team relationships and dynamic:

- How do you ensure clear decision making, delegation and communication?
- How do you trip yourselves up at the moment?
- How effective are you in holding each other accountable for delivering your shared goals?
- How do you handle conflict and tension? What needs to shift?
- What is not said in this team?
- What unique qualities do you each bring?
- How well do you use your diverse styles to deliver optimum value to the business?
- What do you need to shift in your dynamic of working together?

Collective leadership capability:

- How well do you engage the next level of leadership in creating and delivering your agenda?
- How do you ensure you are seen as one integrated team in providing leadership?
- What needs to shift in your leadership for you to role-model the business you aspire to be?
- What needs to shift in your relationship with others in a leadership position (for example, the chair and the board)?
- What needs to shift in your relationship with key customers, suppliers, other stakeholders?
- How do you manage the tensions in the organisation structure so that there is creative tension rather than dysfunctional tension?

Team growth and learning:

- What time do you currently give to learning from your experience and building that into your ways of working?
- How well do you support the growth of team members?
- What works well and what needs to shift?

Example Inquiry Questions for the Team's Primary Stakeholders
(Adapt the questions for other stakeholders)

Primary stakeholder's commission to the team:

- What are the key external challenges that the business faces currently and in the next two to five years?
- What do you need from the team to respond to these challenges?
- What does the team do well?
- What needs to shift in your view?
- What are the strengths of your relationship with the team and what needs to shift to create enhanced clarity of purpose, partnership and shared leadership?

Strategy, purpose, role:

- How far does the team have a clear strategy to fulfil its vision and purpose?
- How far are the purpose, vision and strategy jointly owned by the whole team?
- What needs to shift for the team to execute their strategy more effectively?

Team relationships and dynamics from your perspective:

- How well does the team work together?
- How effective are they in holding each other accountable for delivering shared goals?
- How well does the team handle conflict and tension? What needs to shift?
- What is not said in this team?
- What unique qualities do team members bring?
- How well does the team use its diverse styles to deliver optimum value to the business?
- What needs to shift in the team dynamic for it to perform more effectively?

Collective leadership capability:

- How well does the team engage the next level of leadership in creating and delivering its agenda?
- How far is it seen as one integrated team in providing leadership?
- What needs to shift in its leadership – with primary stakeholders? With direct reports? With staff? With other stakeholders – key customers, suppliers?
- How well does the team manage the tensions in the organisation structure so that there is creative tension rather than dysfunctional tension?

Team growth and learning:

- How does this team learn from its experience and build that into their ways of working?
- How well does it support the growth of team members?
- What works well and what needs to shift?

If there was one request you would have of this team, what would it be?